Next.js 15

for

Developers

The complete Guide to Server-Side Rendering, API
Development, and Full-Stack Web Apps.

By
KENJI AYA

Table of Contents

Part 1: Getting Started with Next.js 15

Chapter 1: Introduction to Next.js 15

1.1 What is Next.js?

Next.js is a powerful React framework that enables developers to build modern web applications with server-side rendering (SSR), static site generation (SSG), and hybrid rendering capabilities. It provides a seamless developer experience with built-in support for TypeScript, API routes, image optimization, and middleware.

Unlike traditional React applications, which rely on client-side rendering (CSR) and often suffer from **performance bottlenecks and SEO challenges**, Next.js offers an optimized approach by handling rendering on the server, reducing page load times and improving **search engine optimization (SEO).**

Key Benefits of Next.js
- **Hybrid Rendering:** Supports **server-side rendering (SSR), static site generation (SSG), and client-side rendering (CSR)** within the same application.
- **API Routes:** Enables developers to create full-stack applications with **built-in API endpoints.**
- **Automatic Code Splitting:** Loads only the necessary JavaScript for each page, improving performance.
- **Image Optimization:** Optimizes images automatically for faster loading and better user experience.
- **Internationalization (i18n):** Built-in support for multilingual applications.

- **Middleware and Edge Functions:** Enhances performance and enables custom request handling at the edge.

Next.js is used by top companies such as **Netflix, Vercel, Twitch, and GitHub** due to its **scalability, performance, and developer-friendly ecosystem.**

1.2 Key Features of Next.js 15

Next.js 15 introduces several **new features and improvements** over previous versions. This release focuses on **performance, enhanced developer experience, and expanded capabilities for full-stack development.**

New Features in Next.js 15

1. Optimized Server Components

Next.js 15 enhances **React Server Components (RSC)** by improving how components are streamed and hydrated, leading to **faster page loads and better user experiences.**

- **Faster data fetching:** Reduces time-to-first-byte (TTFB) by optimizing SSR.

- **Reduced client-side JavaScript:** Minimizes the bundle size, improving performance.

2. Enhanced Middleware and Edge Functions

Middleware in Next.js 15 allows developers to **intercept and modify requests before they reach the backend.** This enables:

- **Dynamic authentication checks** before rendering a page.

- **Custom headers and redirects** based on user requests.

- **Improved caching strategies** for better performance.

3. Improved API Routes and Server Actions
Next.js 15 enhances API routes with:
- **Streaming responses** for handling real-time data efficiently.
- **Server Actions** that allow better form handling and state management.
- **Optimized database connections** with built-in connection pooling.

4. Advanced Image and Asset Optimization
- **Native AVIF support:** Improves image compression without sacrificing quality.
- **Smarter lazy loading:** Ensures images load when needed, reducing initial load time.

5. Seamless Integration with AI and LLM APIs
- Built-in support for **OpenAI, DeepSeek, and other AI-powered APIs** to enhance Next.js applications.

These updates make Next.js 15 **one of the most advanced frameworks for full-stack web development.**

1.3 Why Choose Next.js for Modern Web Development?

Modern web applications require **speed, security, scalability, and flexibility.** Next.js is a preferred choice for many developers due to its ability to **seamlessly integrate frontend and backend capabilities.**

Key Advantages of Next.js in Real-World Projects

Feature	Benefit

Server-Side Rendering (SSR)	Improves SEO and performance by generating content on the server.
Static Site Generation (SSG)	Pre-renders pages at build time, making them fast and efficient.
Incremental Static Regeneration (ISR)	Updates static content without rebuilding the entire site.
Full-Stack Capabilities	Built-in API routes allow seamless backend integration.
Optimized Performance	Automatic code-splitting, image optimization, and lazy loading.
Scalability	Works for startups and enterprise-level applications.

Who Should Use Next.js?

- **Frontend Developers:** Who want to move beyond React and explore full-stack capabilities.
- **Backend Developers:** Looking for an efficient way to integrate APIs and database operations.
- **Startup Teams:** Needing a scalable, high-performance framework with rapid deployment.
- **SEO Specialists:** Optimizing for better rankings in Google search.

Next.js provides **out-of-the-box solutions** that save developers time while ensuring **modern web best practices.**

1.4 Understanding the Evolution from Next.js 14 to 15

With every new version, Next.js introduces **improvements in speed, efficiency, and developer experience.**

Key Improvements from Next.js 14 to 15

Feature	Next.js 14	Next.js 15
React Server Components (RSC)	Introduced	Optimized for faster rendering
Middleware	Experimental	Fully stable and production-ready
Edge Functions	Limited use cases	Expanded functionality and performance
API Routes	Standard support	Streaming and Server Actions for real-time data
Image Optimization	Basic AVIF support	Native AVIF and improved lazy loading
AI & LLM API Support	Manual integration	Built-in support for AI-driven applications

These enhancements make **Next.js 15 the most powerful version yet,** bringing increased speed, flexibility, and scalability.

Chapter 2: Setting Up Your Development Environment

Before diving into Next.js 15 development, it is essential to set up a robust and efficient development environment. This chapter will guide you through installing Node.js, creating a new Next.js project, understanding the default project structure, and running the development server. By the end of this chapter, you will have a fully functional Next.js setup, ready for building modern full-stack applications.

2.1 Installing Node.js and npm

Before you can start building applications with Next.js 15, you need to install **Node.js** and its package manager, **npm**. Node.js provides the JavaScript runtime that allows you to execute JavaScript outside the browser, while npm (Node Package Manager) is used to manage dependencies for JavaScript applications.

This section will guide you through:

- Understanding why Node.js and npm are necessary for Next.js development

- Checking if Node.js is already installed on your system

- Installing Node.js and npm on Windows, macOS, and Linux

- Verifying   the   installation

2.1.1 Why Do You Need Node.js and npm?

Next.js is a **React-based framework** that relies on **server-side rendering (SSR)**, **static site generation (SSG)**, and **API routes**, all of which require a **JavaScript runtime** to execute code outside the browser. Node.js serves as this runtime, enabling features such as:

- Running Next.js development and production servers

- Handling server-side logic for API routes

- Executing JavaScript on the backend

npm (or an alternative package manager like Yarn or pnpm) is essential for:

- Installing Next.js and its dependencies

- Managing third-party libraries

- Running scripts to build and deploy your application

Without Node.js and npm, you cannot set up a Next.js project or run its development environment.

2.1.2 Checking If Node.js Is Installed

Before installing Node.js, check if it is already installed on your system.

Step 1: Open a Terminal

Depending on your operating system:

- **Windows:** Open **Command Prompt (cmd)** or **PowerShell**

- **macOS:** Open **Terminal**

- **Linux:** Open **Terminal**

Step 2: Check the Installed Node.js Version

Run the following command:

sh

```
node -v
```

If Node.js is installed, this command will return a version number, such as:

sh

```
v18.17.1
```

If you see an error like `"command not found"` or `"node is not recognized"`, Node.js is not installed on your system.

Step 3: Check the Installed npm Version

Run:

sh

```
npm -v
```

This should return a version number, such as:

```
sh
```

```
9.6.0
```

If npm is missing, reinstall Node.js because npm comes bundled with it.

2.1.3 Installing Node.js and npm

If Node.js is not installed, follow the steps below to install it based on your operating system.

Installing on Windows and macOS

1. **Download Node.js**

   ○ Go to the official website: https://nodejs.org

   ○ Download the **LTS (Long-Term Support) version**, as it ensures better stability and compatibility.

2. **Run the Installer**

   ○ Open the downloaded file (`.msi` for Windows, `.pkg` for macOS).

   ○ Follow the installation wizard and accept the default settings.

3. **Verify the Installation**

   ○ Open a new terminal or command prompt.

Run:
sh

```
node -v
```

```
npm -v
```

4. If both commands return version numbers, the installation was successful.

Installing on Linux

There are multiple ways to install Node.js on Linux. The recommended method is using **Node Version Manager (nvm)** for flexibility.

Method 1: Using nvm (Recommended)

Install nvm:

sh
```
curl -fsSL
https://raw.githubusercontent.com/nvm-
sh/nvm/v0.39.4/install.sh | bash
```

Reload the terminal configuration:

sh
```
source ~/.bashrc   # or ~/.zshrc if using zsh
```

Install the latest LTS version of Node.js:

sh
```
nvm install --lts
```

Verify installation:

```sh
node -v

npm -v
```

This method allows you to switch between different Node.js versions easily.

Method 2: Using the System Package Manager

If you prefer to install Node.js directly using your system's package manager:

Debian/Ubuntu:

```sh
sudo apt update

sudo apt install -y nodejs npm
```

Fedora:
```sh
sudo dnf install -y nodejs npm
```

Arch Linux:
```sh
sudo pacman -S nodejs npm
```

After installation, verify using:

sh

```
node -v

npm -v
```

2.1.4 Upgrading Node.js and npm

To ensure compatibility with Next.js 15, keep Node.js and npm updated.

Updating Node.js

If you installed Node.js via nvm, update it using:

sh

```
nvm install --lts
```

- If you installed Node.js via the official installer, download the latest version from https://nodejs.org and run the installer again.

Updating npm

To update npm to the latest version, run:

sh

```
npm install -g npm
```

Verify the update:

sh

```
npm -v
```

2.1.5 Alternative Package Managers: Yarn and pnpm

npm is the default package manager for Node.js, but some developers prefer alternative package managers like **Yarn** and **pnpm** for performance improvements and additional features.

Installing Yarn

Yarn is an alternative to npm that improves dependency resolution speed. To install it:

sh

```
npm install -g yarn
```

Verify installation:

sh

```
yarn -v
```

Installing pnpm

pnpm is another package manager optimized for efficiency and disk space usage. To install it:

sh

```
npm install -g pnpm
```

Verify installation:

sh

```
pnpm -v
```

Both package managers are fully compatible with Next.js. You can use them instead of npm when creating and managing projects.

2.2 Creating a New Next.js Project

Now that you have installed **Node.js** and **npm** (or an alternative package manager), you are ready to create a **Next.js 15** project. This section will guide you through:

- Understanding how a Next.js project is structured

- Creating a Next.js project using `create-next-app`

- Exploring key project files and directories

- Running the development server

2.2.1 Understanding Next.js Project Structure

A Next.js project consists of multiple folders and files that help manage routes, components, styles, and backend logic efficiently. Before diving into the setup, here is an overview of what a typical **Next.js 15** project looks like:

ruby

```
my-next-app/

|— app/          # App Router (for layouts and pages)

|— components/    # Reusable UI components

|— public/       # Static assets (images, icons, etc.)

|— styles/       # Global styles (CSS, SCSS, etc.)

|— next.config.js  # Next.js configuration file

|— package.json   # Project metadata and dependencies

|— .gitignore     # Git ignored files

|— README.md      # Project documentation
```

Understanding this structure will help you navigate the project effectively once it is created.

2.2.2 Creating a Next.js Project Using `create-next-app`

The easiest and recommended way to create a **Next.js 15** project is by using `create-next-app`. This command sets up a fully functional Next.js project with the latest best practices and configurations.

Step 1: Open a Terminal

Ensure you have a terminal or command prompt open before proceeding.

Step 2: Run the `create-next-app` Command

Run the following command to create a new Next.js project:

sh

```
npx create-next-app@latest my-next-app
```

Breaking Down the Command

- `npx` – Executes the `create-next-app` package without installing it globally

- `create-next-app@latest` – Ensures you are using the latest version of the Next.js project generator

- `my-next-app` – The name of your project (you can change this to any preferred name)

Alternative: Using Yarn or pnpm

23

If you are using **Yarn**, run:

sh

```
yarn create next-app my-next-app
```

If you are using **pnpm**, run:

sh

```
pnpm create next-app my-next-app
```

2.2.3 Configuring the Project Setup

When running `create-next-app`, you will be prompted to customize your setup with the following options:

sh

✓ Would you like to use TypeScript with this project? › (y/N)

✓ Would you like to use ESLint? › (y/N)

✓ Would you like to use Tailwind CSS? › (y/N)

✓ Would you like to use `src/` directory? › (y/N)

✓ Would you like to use experimental `app/` directory with App Router? › (y/N)

✓ What import alias would you like configured? › @/*

Recommended Configuration

For this book, select the following options:

- **TypeScript:** Yes (recommended for scalability and type safety)

- **ESLint:** Yes (recommended for maintaining clean code)

- **Tailwind CSS:** No (optional, but we will cover styling separately)

- src/ **directory:** No (we will keep a simpler project structure)

- **Experimental** app/ **directory:** Yes (this enables the App Router, which is the default in Next.js 15)

- **Import alias:** Keep the default @ / *

After selecting these options, Next.js will generate the necessary files and install dependencies.

2.2.4 Navigating Your Next.js Project

Once the setup is complete, navigate to your project directory:

sh

```
cd my-next-app
```

Your Next.js project will include the following key files:

- `package.json` – Contains project metadata and dependencies

- `next.config.js` – Configuration settings for Next.js

- `app/` – The new App Router directory, managing layouts and routes

- `pages/` (if using the Pages Router) – Traditional Next.js routing system

- `public/` – Stores static assets such as images

To view the default **dependencies**, check the `package.json` file:

json

```json
{

  "dependencies": {

    "next": "^15.0.0",

    "react": "^18.2.0",

    "react-dom": "^18.2.0"

  }

}
```

These dependencies ensure your Next.js project runs smoothly with React 18.

2.2.5 Running the Next.js Development Server

To start the development server, run:

sh

```
npm run dev
```

If using Yarn:

sh

```
yarn dev
```

Or with pnpm:

sh

```
pnpm dev
```

This will output something like:

sh

```
Local: http://localhost:3000
```

Accessing Your Project

1. Open a browser and navigate to `http://localhost:3000`

2. You should see the default Next.js welcome page

This means your Next.js project has been successfully set up and is running in development mode.

2.2.6 Understanding the Development Workflow

With the project set up, you can now:

- Modify files in the `app/` directory to create pages

- Update **global styles** in the `styles/` folder

- Install additional dependencies using `npm install <package>`

- Restart the development server when needed using `npm run dev`

Next.js supports **hot reloading**, meaning any changes you make will automatically reflect in the browser without needing a manual refresh.

2.3 Understanding Project Structure

Now that you have successfully created a **Next.js 15** project, it is essential to understand its structure. The default project setup includes a well-organized directory layout that facilitates **scalability, maintainability, and efficient development**.

In this section, you will learn:

- The key directories and files in a Next.js project

- The purpose of each file and how it contributes to your application

- The difference between the **App Router (app/ directory)** and the **Pages Router (pages/ directory)**

- How to organize your project for real-world applications

2.3.1 Overview of a Next.js 15 Project Structure

After creating a Next.js project with create-next-app, your directory structure will look like this:

ruby

```
my-next-app/

|— app/          # App Router (manages layouts and pages)

|— components/   # Reusable UI components

|— public/       # Static assets (images, icons, etc.)

|— styles/       # Global styles (CSS, SCSS, etc.)

|— next.config.js  # Next.js configuration file

|— package.json    # Project metadata and dependencies
```

```
|— .gitignore      # Git ignored files

|— README.md       # Project documentation
```

Let's break down each directory and file in detail.

2.3.2 Key Directories and Their Purpose

1. app/ (App Router - Recommended in Next.js 15)

The app/ directory is the foundation of Next.js's new **App Router** system, which improves server-side rendering and layouts.

Inside app/, you will typically find:

bash

```
app/

|— layout.tsx      # Defines the layout for all pages

|— page.tsx        # The main entry point (homepage)

|— about/          # Example subdirectory for a page

|     |— page.tsx    # Renders the About page
```

```
|─ dashboard/       # Example dynamic section

│   ├─ layout.tsx   # Dashboard layout

│   ├─ page.tsx     # Dashboard home page

│   ├─ settings/    # Nested settings page

│       ├─ page.tsx
```

Key Features of the app/ **Directory:**

- Uses **React   Server   Components**   by   default

- Supports **layouts and nested layouts** for structuring UI

- Improves **performance** by enabling server-side rendering efficiently

- Allows for **loading, error, and metadata** handling in a structured   way

Note: If you selected the pages/ directory during setup, you will be using the **Pages Router** instead of the **App Router**. However, the App Router is the recommended approach for Next.js 15.

2. `components/` (Reusable UI Components)

This directory stores reusable **React components** such as buttons, headers, footers, and form elements.

Example structure:

bash

```
components/

|—— Navbar.tsx      # Navigation bar component

|—— Footer.tsx      # Footer component

|—— Card.tsx        # UI card component
```

Storing components separately improves code organization and reusability.

---

3. `public/` (Static Assets)

The `public/` directory is used for storing **static assets** such as images, icons, and fonts.

- Files inside `public/` are **accessible directly via the browser**

- Example: `public/logo.png` can be accessed using `/logo.png`

Example structure:

php

```
public/
│── favicon.ico     # Favicon for the website
│── logo.png        # Logo image
│── images/         # Folder for additional images
│    ├── banner.jpg
│    ├── profile.jpg
```

---

4. `styles/` (Global Styles & CSS Modules)

The `styles/` directory contains global stylesheets and CSS modules.

- **Global styles:** `globals.css` applies styles globally across the app
- **CSS Modules:** Used for component-scoped styles

Example structure:

ruby

```
styles/
│── globals.css     # Global styles
```

|—— Home.module.css # Scoped styles for Home component

|—— Button.module.css # Scoped styles for Button component

Next.js supports multiple styling approaches, including **CSS Modules, Tailwind CSS, and styled-components**.

2.3.3 Key Files in a Next.js Project

1. `next.config.js` **(Next.js Configuration File)**

This file allows you to customize Next.js settings such as:

- **Enabling experimental features**

- **Customizing headers and redirects**

- **Optimizing images**

Example `next.config.js`:

js

```js
/** @type {import('next').NextConfig} */

const nextConfig = {

  reactStrictMode: true,

  images: {

    domains: ['example.com'], // Allow loading images from external domains
```

```
  },

};

module.exports = nextConfig;
```

2. `package.json` (Project Metadata & Dependencies)

This file contains project metadata and dependencies.

Example `package.json`:

json

```
{

  "name": "my-next-app",

  "version": "1.0.0",

  "dependencies": {

    "next": "^15.0.0",

    "react": "^18.2.0",

    "react-dom": "^18.2.0"

  },

  "scripts": {

    "dev": "next dev",
```

```
    "build": "next build",

    "start": "next start"

  }

}
```

3. `.gitignore` (Ignored Files for Git Version Control)

Defines files and directories that should be ignored by Git.

Example `.gitignore`:

bash

```
node_modules

.next/

.env

.DS_Store
```

This prevents unnecessary files from being pushed to a repository.

4. `README.md` (Project Documentation)

This file provides an overview of your project, including setup instructions.

Example:

md

```
# My Next.js App

This is a Next.js 15 project.

## Getting Started

1. Install dependencies: `npm install`

 2. Start the development server: `npm run dev`
```

Writing good documentation ensures better collaboration and maintainability.

2.3.4 Organizing a Next.js Project for Scalability

For **larger projects**, it is important to follow best practices for organization.

Recommended Project Structure for Large Applications

ruby

```
my-next-app/

|— app/          # App Router (layouts and pages)

|— components/     # Reusable UI components

|— hooks/         # Custom React hooks
```

```
|— lib/           # Utility functions and helper modules

|— services/      # API service functions

|— contexts/      # React Context providers

|— styles/        # Global styles and CSS modules

|— public/        # Static assets

|— next.config.js # Configuration

|— package.json   # Project metadata

|— .gitignore     # Ignored files

|— README.md      # Documentation
```

Why This Structure Works Well?

- **Separation of concerns** – UI components, hooks, and logic are modular

- **Easier maintenance** – Large applications remain manageable

- **Scalability** – New features can be added without major refactoring

2.4 Running and Configuring the Development Server

After setting up a Next.js 15 project and understanding its structure, the next step is to run and configure the development server. The **Next.js development server** provides a fast, interactive, and optimized development experience with features like **hot reloading, error overlays, and server-side rendering**.

In this section, you will learn:

- How to start the Next.js development server

- Understanding key development server features

- Customizing the development environment

- Managing environment variables

2.4.1 Starting the Development Server

Next.js provides a built-in development server that allows you to test your application locally with features like **automatic code updates** and **fast refresh**.

To start the development server, navigate to your project directory and run:

Using npm

sh

```
npm run dev
```

Using yarn

sh

```
yarn dev
```

Using pnpm

sh

```
pnpm dev
```

By default, the development server runs at **http://localhost:3000/**. Open this URL in a web browser to see your application in action.

Note: If port 3000 is already in use, Next.js will automatically find another available port (e.g., 3001, 3002). You can also specify a custom port manually (covered in section **2.4.3**).

2.4.2 Key Features of the Development Server

The Next.js development server comes with several built-in features that enhance the development experience.

1. Fast Refresh

Fast Refresh allows you to see changes immediately without losing component state.

- When editing **React components**, updates are applied instantly.

- For **server-side changes**, Next.js reloads the page to reflect updates.

Example: Modify a component in `app/page.tsx` and see the update in real time without refreshing the browser manually.

2. Automatic Routing

Next.js automatically generates routes based on the project structure.

- `app/page.tsx` → `Available at /`

- `app/about/page.tsx` → `Available at /about`

- `app/dashboard/page.tsx` → `Available at /dashboard`

This eliminates the need for manual route configuration.

3. Error Overlays

If an error occurs in the development environment, Next.js provides an **interactive error overlay** in the browser.

Example error:

js
```
ReferenceError: myVariable is not defined
```

Instead of a blank screen, you will see an overlay with:

- The **error message**

- The **file and line number** where the error occurred

- Suggestions on how to fix the issue

This feature makes debugging more efficient.

---

4. API Route Hot Reloading

If you modify an **API route** inside app/api/, Next.js will automatically reload only the affected API file without restarting the entire server.

Example:

Modify app/api/hello/route.ts

ts
```ts
export async function GET() {
  return new Response("Hello, Next.js 15!", {
status: 200 });
}
```

Changes will reflect instantly when you make a request to /api/hello.

2.4.3 Configuring the Development Server

Next.js allows you to customize the development server settings based on your needs.

1. Running the Server on a Custom Port

By default, the Next.js development server runs on **port 3000**, but you can specify a custom port.

Example: Run the server on **port 4000**

```sh
npm run dev -- -p 4000
```

or

```sh
next dev -p 4000
```

Now, your application will be accessible at **http://localhost:4000/**.

2. Enabling HTTPS for Local Development

By default, the Next.js development server runs on HTTP, but you can enable HTTPS using a self-signed certificate.

To use HTTPS with a local certificate, run:

```sh
next dev -- -p 3000 --https
```

Note: You need to generate SSL certificates and specify them using `NODE_EXTRA_CA_CERTS` or a proxy tool like **mkcert**.

---

3. Customizing the Host

By default, the server binds to `localhost`, but you can specify a different host.

Example: Run on **0.0.0.0** to allow access from other devices in the network.

sh
```
next dev -H 0.0.0.0 -p 3000
```

Now, the application is accessible from other devices using your machine's IP address.

2.4.4 Managing Environment Variables

Next.js supports **environment variables** to store sensitive information like API keys and database credentials.

1. Creating an Environment File (`.env.local`)

Inside your Next.js project root, create a `.env.local` file:

ini
```
NEXT_PUBLIC_API_URL=https://api.example.com
DATABASE_URL=postgres://user:password@localho
st:5432/mydb
```

Important: Variables prefixed with `NEXT_PUBLIC_` are exposed to the client, while others remain server-side only.

2. Accessing Environment Variables in Code

Next.js provides the `process.env` object to access environment variables.

Example:

ts
```
const                    apiUrl                  =
process.env.NEXT_PUBLIC_API_URL;

export default function HomePage() {
  return <p>API URL: {apiUrl}</p>;
}
```

3. Loading Environment Variables in API Routes

Example API route using an environment variable:

ts
```
export async function GET() {
  const dbUrl = process.env.DATABASE_URL;
  return    new    Response(`Database    URL:
${dbUrl}`, { status: 200 });
}
```

Note: Restart the server after modifying environment variables to apply changes.

2.4.5 Debugging and Optimizing the Development Workflow

To streamline development, consider using the following techniques:

1. Debugging with Console Logs

Insert `console.log` statements inside components or API routes:

ts
```
console.log("Fetching data...");
```

View logs directly in the **browser console** or **terminal output**.

2. Using Next.js Debug Mode

Enable verbose logs for troubleshooting:

sh
```
NEXT_DEBUG=1 npm run dev
```

This provides additional insights into server-side processes.

3. Restarting the Development Server

If you encounter issues like **stale environment variables**, restart the server:

sh
```
npm run dev
```

or use:

```sh
rs
```

inside the terminal.

Chapter 3: Understanding Pages and Routing

Routing is a fundamental part of any web application, defining how users navigate between pages and access different parts of the application. In Next.js 15, routing is **file-based**, meaning that the structure of the app/ directory determines the application's URL structure.

This chapter covers:

- **File-based routing** and how Next.js automatically maps files to URLs

- **Dynamic routes and catch-all routes** for handling variable paths

- **Navigating between pages** using next/link for seamless transitions

- **Middleware and API route handlers** for customizing request handling

---

3.1 File-Based Routing in Next.js

Routing is a fundamental concept in any web framework, determining how users navigate between different pages in an application. In Next.js, **routing is based on the file system**—each file inside the app/ directory automatically becomes a route. This **file-based routing system** simplifies development by eliminating the need for manual route configuration.

In this section, we will explore:

- **How file-based routing works** in Next.js

- **Creating pages** and understanding the app/ directory

- **Nested routes and layouts** for structuring applications

3.1.1 Understanding the File-Based Routing System

Next.js 15 uses the **app/ directory** as the foundation for its routing system. Each file within this directory corresponds to a URL path.

For example, consider the following folder structure:

bash

```
app/
├── page.tsx          → /
├── about/
│   ├── page.tsx      → /about
├── contact/
│   ├── page.tsx      → /contact
```

- The app/page.tsx file corresponds to the **homepage** (/).

- The app/about/page.tsx file corresponds to /about.

- The app/contact/page.tsx file corresponds to /contact.

Each of these files automatically becomes a route, making the development process straightforward and intuitive.

3.1.2 Creating Your First Page

To create a basic page in Next.js, simply add a `page.tsx` file inside the `app/` directory.

Example: Creating `app/page.tsx` (Homepage)

tsx

```
export default function HomePage() {
  return <h1>Welcome to Next.js 15</h1>;
}
```

How It Works:

- The function `HomePage` returns a simple `<h1>` heading.

- Next.js automatically serves this page at **http://localhost:3000/** when running the development server.

3.1.3 Nested Routes in Next.js

A subdirectory inside `app/` creates a **nested route**.

Example: Creating `app/about/page.tsx`

tsx

```
export default function AboutPage() {
  return <h1>About Us</h1>;
```

```
}
```

How It Works:

- This file corresponds to the `/about` route.

- Visiting **http://localhost:3000/about** will display the "About Us" page.

3.1.4 Using Layouts for Consistent Structure

Next.js allows defining **layouts** that wrap around all pages, providing a consistent structure.

Creating a Global Layout

A `layout.tsx` file inside `app/` defines a **global layout** for the entire application.

Example: Creating `app/layout.tsx`

tsx
```tsx
export default function RootLayout({ children
}: { children: React.ReactNode }) {
  return (
    <html lang="en">
      <body>
        <nav>
          <a    href="/">Home</a>    |    <a
href="/about">About</a>
        </nav>
        {children}
      </body>
```

```
    </html>
  );
}
```

How It Works:

- The `layout.tsx` file wraps every page in the application.

- The `<nav>` bar is shared across all pages.

- The `{children}` placeholder ensures that each individual page's content is rendered inside the layout.

Now, every page will include the **navigation bar** automatically.

3.2 Dynamic Routes and Catch-All Routes

Static routes in Next.js work well for predefined pages, but dynamic routes allow flexibility by handling multiple URL variations using a single file. This is useful for **blogs, user profiles, product pages, and other dynamic content-driven applications**.

In this section, we will cover:

- **Dynamic routes** in Next.js

- **Using URL parameters** in dynamic pages

- **Catch-all routes** for handling multiple URL segments

- **Optional   catch-all   routes**   for   more   flexibility

3.2.1 Understanding Dynamic Routes

A **dynamic route** is created by **wrapping a filename in square brackets [ ]** inside the app/ directory.

Example: Creating a Dynamic Route for User Profiles

Consider an application with user profile pages at /users/john, /users/alex, etc. Instead of creating separate files for each user, we define a **dynamic route**:

Folder Structure

bash

```
app/
 ├── users/
 │    ├── [username]/
 │    │    ├── page.tsx   → /users/:username
```

Dynamic Route Page: app/users/[username]/page.tsx

tsx

```tsx
interface Params {
  params: { username: string };
}

export default function UserProfile({ params
}: Params) {
  return <h1>Welcome, {params.username}</h1>;
}
```

How It Works:

- The `[username]` folder makes this route **dynamic**, allowing any `username` value in the URL.

- The `params` object extracts the `username` from the URL.

- Accessing `/users/john` will render: **"Welcome, john"**.

- Accessing `/users/alex` will render: **"Welcome, alex"**.

3.2.2 Catch-All Routes

A **catch-all route** captures multiple URL segments. This is useful for handling **nested categories, blog posts, or deeply structured URLs**.

Example: Creating a Catch-All Route for Blog Posts

Consider a blog with categories like `/blog/tech/javascript` or `/blog/travel/europe/italy`. Instead of creating separate routes, we use a **catch-all route**:

Folder Structure

bash

```
app/
 ├── blog/
 │    ├── [...slug]/
 │    │     ├── page.tsx    → /blog/:slug (supports multiple
segments)
```

Catch-All Route Page: `app/blog/[...slug]/page.tsx`

tsx

```tsx
interface Params {
  params: { slug: string[] };
}

export default function BlogPost({ params }:
Params) {
  return (
    <div>
      <h1>Blog  Path:  {params.slug.join("  /
")}</h1>
    </div>
  );
}
```

How It Works:

- The `[...slug]` notation allows multiple path segments.

- The `params.slug` array stores each segment of the URL.

- Accessing `/blog/tech/javascript` will render: **"Blog Path: tech / javascript"**.

- Accessing `/blog/travel/europe/italy` will render: **"Blog Path: travel / europe / italy"**.

3.2.3 Optional Catch-All Routes

An **optional catch-all route** behaves like a normal route when no additional segments are provided but can also handle extra segments.

Example: Handling Optional Blog Categories

lua

```
app/
 ├── blog/
 │    ├── [[...slug]]/
 │    │    ├── page.tsx  → /blog/ (optional segments)
```

Optional   Catch-All   Route   Page: app/blog/[[...slug]]/page.tsx

tsx

```tsx
interface Params {
  params: { slug?: string[] };
}

export default function BlogPage({ params }:
Params) {
  const    path    =    params.slug    ?
params.slug.join(" / ") : "Home";

  return (
    <div>
      <h1>Blog Section: {path}</h1>
    </div>
```

```
  );
}
```

How It Works:

- The `[[...slug]]` notation makes the segments **optional**.

- If no segments are provided, the page renders a default message.

- Accessing `/blog/` renders **"Blog Section: Home"**.

- Accessing `/blog/tech` renders **"Blog Section: tech"**.

3.3 Navigating Between Pages with next/link

Navigation is a fundamental aspect of any web application. In Next.js, the `next/link` component provides an efficient way to navigate between pages while optimizing performance. Unlike traditional `<a>` tags that cause full-page reloads, `next/link` enables client-side transitions, improving the user experience by keeping state and reducing load times.

In this section, we will cover:

- Understanding client-side navigation with `next/link`

- Implementing basic navigation between pages

- Using dynamic route parameters in navigation

- Enhancing navigation with custom styling and active states

3.3.1 Understanding Client-Side Navigation with `next/link`

Next.js uses a **file-based routing system**, where each file inside the `app/` directory corresponds to a route. While you can navigate between these pages using standard `<a>` tags, this approach causes full-page reloads, losing application state and causing unnecessary delays.

Instead, Next.js provides `next/link`, which enables **instant, client-side navigation** while maintaining state and improving performance.

How `next/link` Works

The `next/link` component prefetches linked pages in the background (when enabled), allowing near-instant navigation. This is particularly useful for **Single Page Applications (SPAs)** and **server-side rendered (SSR) applications**.

3.3.2 Implementing Basic Navigation Between Pages

To demonstrate navigation, let's create two pages:

- `app/index.tsx` (Home Page)

- `app/about/page.tsx` (About Page)

Folder Structure

bash

`app/`

```
├── page.tsx    → /
├── about/
│   ├── page.tsx → /about
```

Home Page (`app/page.tsx`)

tsx
```tsx
import Link from "next/link";

export default function Home() {
  return (
    <div>
      <h1>Welcome to My Next.js App</h1>
      <p>Click the link below to visit the
About page:</p>
      <Link    href="/about">Go    to    About
Page</Link>
    </div>
  );
}
```

About Page (`app/about/page.tsx`)

tsx

```tsx
export default function About() {
  return (
    <div>
      <h1>About Us</h1>
      <p>This is the About page.</p>
    </div>
  );
```

```
}
```

Now, clicking on **"Go to About Page"** will navigate to /about **without a full-page reload**.

3.3.3 Using Dynamic Route Parameters in Navigation

When working with **dynamic routes**, you often need to pass parameters in links. Next.js allows this by embedding dynamic values in href.

Example: Navigating to a User Profile

Assume we have a dynamic route for user profiles:

```bash
app/
 ├── users/
 │    ├── [username]/
 │    │    ├── page.tsx  → /users/:username
```

Creating the User Profile Page (app/users/[username]/page.tsx)

```tsx
interface Params {
  params: { username: string };
}
export default function UserProfile({ params
}: Params) {
  return <h1>Welcome, {params.username}</h1>;
}
```

Linking to a Dynamic User Page

tsx

```tsx
import Link from "next/link";

export default function UsersPage() {
  return (
    <div>
      <h1>Users</h1>
      <ul>
        <li>
          <Link       href="/users/john">John's
Profile</Link>
        </li>
        <li>
          <Link       href="/users/alex">Alex's
Profile</Link>
        </li>
      </ul>
    </div>
  );
}
```

Clicking on **"John's Profile"** will navigate to `/users/john`, rendering the UserProfile component.

3.3.4 Enhancing Navigation with Custom Styling and Active States

By default, `next/link` does not apply styles to the active link. However, you can enhance navigation by:

- Styling the active link

- Wrapping `next/link` inside a `<nav>`

- Using `usePathname()` from `next/navigation` to detect active routes

Example: Highlighting the Active Link

tsx

```tsx
"use client";
import Link from "next/link";
import { usePathname } from "next/navigation";

export default function Navbar() {
  const pathname = usePathname();

  return (
    <nav>
      <Link href="/" className={pathname ===
"/" ? "active" : ""}>
        Home
      </Link>
      <Link href="/about" className={pathname
=== "/about" ? "active" : ""}>
        About
      </Link>
      <style jsx>{`
        nav {
          display: flex;
          gap: 20px;
          padding: 10px;
```

```
      }
      .active {
        font-weight: bold;
        color: blue;
      }
    `}</style>
  </nav>
);
}
```

Now, when a link is active, it will be styled in **bold and blue**.

3.4 Middleware and API Route Handlers

Middleware and API routes in Next.js 15 provide powerful capabilities for handling **custom request processing, authentication, logging, rate-limiting, and API endpoint management**. Middleware enables **intercepting and modifying requests** before they reach a route, while API routes allow for building backend logic within a Next.js application.

In this section, we will cover:

- Understanding middleware in Next.js
- Implementing custom middleware for request handling
- Using API routes for building backend logic
- Handling different HTTP methods in API routes
- Connecting API routes with a database

3.4.1 Understanding Middleware in Next.js

Middleware in Next.js is executed **before a request reaches its final destination**. It allows developers to modify request headers, redirect users, enforce authentication, and log request details.

Middleware runs at the **Edge Runtime**, meaning it executes closer to the user, reducing latency. It is particularly useful for **security checks, A/B testing, feature flagging, and dynamic routing**.

Key Features of Middleware

- **Runs before the request reaches the final handler**

- **Executes at the Edge**, improving performance

- **Can modify requests and responses dynamically**

- **Useful for authentication, logging, redirects, and security policies**

3.4.2 Implementing Custom Middleware

To define middleware in Next.js, create a file named `middleware.ts` in the root directory (`app/`).

Example: Redirecting Users Based on Authentication

tsx

```
import { NextRequest, NextResponse } from
"next/server";

export function middleware(req: NextRequest) {
```

```
  const             isAuthenticated              =
req.cookies.get("auth-token");

  if              (!isAuthenticated              &&
req.nextUrl.pathname.startsWith("/dashboard")
) {
    return            NextResponse.redirect(new
URL("/login", req.url));
  }

  return NextResponse.next();
}

export const config = {
  matcher:  ["/dashboard/:path*"],  //  Apply
middleware to /dashboard and its subroutes
};
```

How It Works:

- **Intercepts requests** to /dashboard and its subroutes.

- **Checks for an authentication token** in cookies.

- **Redirects unauthenticated users** to /login.

- **Allows the request to proceed** if authentication is valid.

3.4.3 Using API Routes for Backend Logic

API routes in Next.js allow developers to build **backend functionality** directly within the application. These routes are defined inside the `app/api/` directory and can handle **server-side logic, database queries, authentication, and more**.

Creating an API Route

Define API routes inside `app/api/` using the Next.js **Request & Response handlers**.

Example: Creating a Simple API Route

Folder Structure
bash

```
app/
 ├── api/
 │   ├── hello/
 │   │   ├── route.ts   → Handles API requests at /api/hello
```

API Route (`app/api/hello/route.ts`)
tsx

```tsx
import { NextResponse } from "next/server";

export function GET() {
  return NextResponse.json({ message: "Hello,
Next.js API!" });
}
```

How It Works:

- Defines an API endpoint at `/api/hello`.
- Handles GET requests and returns a JSON response.
- API routes can also handle POST, PUT, and DELETE methods.

3.4.4 Handling Different HTTP Methods in API Routes

Next.js API routes support various HTTP methods. Let's implement a route that handles **creating, reading, updating, and deleting user data**.

Example: CRUD API for Users

Folder Structure

bash

```
app/
├── api/
│   ├── users/
│   │   ├── route.ts  → Handles API requests at /api/users
```

API Route (`app/api/users/route.ts`)

tsx

```tsx
import { NextResponse } from "next/server";

let users = [{ id: 1, name: "John Doe" }];

export function GET() {
  return NextResponse.json(users);
}
```

```
export async function POST(req: Request) {
  const { name } = await req.json();
  const newUser = { id: users.length + 1, name
};
  users.push(newUser);
  return NextResponse.json(newUser, { status:
201 });
}

export async function DELETE(req: Request) {
  const { id } = await req.json();
  users = users.filter(user => user.id !==
id);
  return NextResponse.json({ message: "User
deleted" }, { status: 200 });
}
```

How It Works:

- **GET**: Returns a list of users.
- **POST**: Creates a new user and adds it to the list.
- **DELETE**: Removes a user by ID.

3.4.5 Connecting API Routes with a Database

Next.js API routes can interact with databases to store and retrieve data. In this example, we will connect an API route to a **MongoDB database using Mongoose**.

Example: Connecting an API Route to MongoDB

Install Dependencies

bash

```bash
npm install mongoose
```

Database Connection (`lib/mongodb.ts`)

tsx

```tsx
import mongoose from "mongoose";

const MONGODB_URI = process.env.MONGODB_URI ||
"";

if (!MONGODB_URI) {
  throw new Error("MONGODB_URI is not
defined");
}

export async function connectDB() {
  if (mongoose.connection.readyState >= 1)
return;
  await mongoose.connect(MONGODB_URI);
}
```

Defining a User Model (`models/User.ts`)

tsx

```tsx
import mongoose from "mongoose";

const UserSchema = new mongoose.Schema({
  name: { type: String, required: true },
```

```
});

export const User = mongoose.models.User ||
mongoose.model("User", UserSchema);
```

API Route with MongoDB (`app/api/users/route.ts`)

tsx

```tsx
import { connectDB } from "@/lib/mongodb";
import { User } from "@/models/User";
import { NextResponse } from "next/server";

export async function GET() {
  await connectDB();
  const users = await User.find();
  return NextResponse.json(users);
}

export async function POST(req: Request) {
  await connectDB();
  const { name } = await req.json();
  const newUser = await User.create({ name });
  return NextResponse.json(newUser, { status:
201 });
}
```

How It Works:

- **Connects to MongoDB** using Mongoose.
- **Defines a User schema** with a name field.
- **Handles GET requests** to retrieve users from the database.

- **Handles POST requests** to create new users.

Part 2:
Rendering, Data Fetching, and API Development

Chapter 4: Rendering Strategies in Next.js 15

Rendering strategies in Next.js 15 determine **how and when pages are generated**. The choice of rendering method directly impacts **performance, SEO, and user experience**. Next.js offers multiple rendering strategies:

1. **Static Site Generation (SSG)** – Pre-generates pages at build time.
2. **Server-Side Rendering (SSR)** – Generates pages on each request.
3. **Incremental Static Regeneration (ISR)** – Updates static pages dynamically after deployment.
4. **Hybrid Rendering** – Uses different strategies in different parts of the application.

Understanding these strategies helps in optimizing **performance, scalability, and SEO** for Next.js applications.

4.1 Static Site Generation (SSG)

Introduction to Static Site Generation

Static Site Generation (SSG) is one of the core rendering strategies in Next.js. With SSG, pages are **pre-generated at build time** and served as static files. This results in **blazing-fast performance, better SEO, and reduced server load**, as there is no need to process each request dynamically.

SSG is the best choice when the content:

- Does **not change frequently** (e.g., marketing pages, blogs, product pages).
- Needs to be **highly optimized for speed and SEO**.
- Should be **scalable** with minimal server costs.

Next.js 15 improves SSG by offering a **more efficient build process**, dynamic route handling, and integration with **Incremental Static Regeneration (ISR)** for updates without requiring full rebuilds.

4.1.1 How Static Site Generation Works

With SSG, Next.js generates the HTML for a page **at build time**, storing it as a static file on the server or a CDN. When a user requests the page, the pre-rendered HTML is served instantly, eliminating the need for real-time processing.

How SSG Differs from Other Rendering Strategies

Rendering Strategy	When is the HTML Generated?	Best Use Cases
SSG (Static Site Generation)	**At build time** (before deployment)	Blogs, documentation, marketing pages
SSR (Server-Side Rendering)	**On each request**	Personalized dashboards, frequently changing data
ISR (Incremental Static Regeneration)	**At build time + updates post-deployment**	E-commerce pages, news sites

4.1.2 Implementing Static Site Generation in Next.js

To enable SSG, create a page inside the `app/` directory and use `generateStaticParams` to pre-generate content.

Example: Generating Static Blog Pages

Let's create a simple blog where posts are generated statically.

Step 1: Define Static Routes Using `generateStaticParams`

tsx
```tsx
// app/blog/[id]/page.tsx
import { notFound } from "next/navigation";

// Sample static data
const posts = [
  { id: "1", title: "Understanding Next.js
15", content: "New rendering strategies in
Next.js 15..." },
  { id: "2", title: "Optimizing Performance",
content: "Best practices for fast Next.js
applications..." },
];

// Generate static routes
export function generateStaticParams() {
  return posts.map(post => ({ id: post.id }));
}

// Page Component
```

```
export default function BlogPost({ params }: {
params: { id: string } }) {
  const  post  =  posts.find(p  =>  p.id  ===
params.id);

  if (!post) return notFound();

  return (
    <div>
      <h1>{post.title}</h1>
      <p>{post.content}</p>
    </div>
  );
}
```

How It Works:

- generateStaticParams runs **at build time**, creating
  static pages for all blog posts.

- The params object fetches the correct post based on the URL.

- If the post ID does not exist, notFound() triggers a **404
  error page**.

Step 2: Running the Build Process

To generate static pages, run the following command:

sh
```
npm run build
```

Next.js will:

- Pre-render pages for each blog post.
- Store them as static files, ready to be served instantly.

4.1.3 Fetching External Data for SSG

SSG is not limited to hardcoded data. You can fetch content from an **external API** at build time.

Example: Fetching Products from an API

tsx

```
// app/products/page.tsx
async function getProducts() {
  const          res          =          await
fetch("https://fakestoreapi.com/products");
  return res.json();
}

export default async function ProductsPage() {
  const products = await getProducts();

  return (
    <div>
      <h1>Products</h1>
      <ul>
        {products.map((product: any) => (
          <li
key={product.id}>{product.title}</li>
        ))}
      </ul>
    </div>
```

```
  );
}
```

How It Works:

- `getProducts()` fetches data **during the build process**.
- The static page is pre-rendered **with the fetched data**.
- All users see the same pre-generated content.

Advantages:

- Improves performance by avoiding database/API requests on every page load.
- Reduces backend load.
- Ensures a **consistent user experience** for all visitors.

4.1.4 Optimizing SSG with Incremental Static Regeneration (ISR)

A major limitation of SSG is that the content is **fixed at build time**. If the data changes frequently, a full rebuild is required. **Incremental Static Regeneration (ISR)** solves this issue by allowing **partial updates** to static pages **without rebuilding the entire site**.

Example: Using ISR to Revalidate Data

tsx

```tsx
// app/api/products/route.ts
import { NextResponse } from "next/server";
export async function GET() {
  const res = await fetch("https://fakestoreapi.com/products");
```

```
const products = await res.json();
return      NextResponse.json(products,      {
revalidate: 60 }); // Updates every 60s
}
```

How It Works:

- The page is **pre-rendered at build time**.
- If a user requests the page after **60 seconds**, Next.js fetches new data **in the background**.
- Users see updated content **without waiting for a full rebuild**.

4.1.5 When to Use Static Site Generation

SSG is ideal for:

Landing pages that don't change often. **Blogs and news articles** where new content is added periodically. **E-commerce product pages** that don't require frequent updates. **Documentation sites** where performance and SEO are key.

Avoid SSG if:

The content changes frequently and requires real-time updates. You need **personalized** data for each user (e.g., dashboards). SEO is not a priority (client-side rendering might be better).

4.2 Server-Side Rendering (SSR)

Server-Side Rendering (SSR) in Next.js allows pages to be **dynamically generated on the server for each request**. This ensures that users always receive **fresh, up-to-date content**, making it an excellent choice for **dynamic applications** where the data changes frequently.

SSR is especially useful when:

- Content must be **personalized** per user request.
- The page data **changes frequently** and must always be current.
- Search Engine Optimization (**SEO**) is important, but static generation (**SSG**) is not feasible due to real-time data needs.

Next.js 15 improves SSR with **enhanced performance optimizations**, **streaming capabilities**, and **better caching mechanisms**, making it an efficient choice for dynamic applications.

4.2.1 How Server-Side Rendering Works

With SSR, when a request is made:

1. The **server processes the request**, fetches necessary data, and generates HTML.
2. The HTML is sent to the **client**, ensuring that the page is fully rendered when it arrives.
3. The **hydration process** takes over, making the page interactive with React.

SSR vs. Other Rendering Strategies

Rendering Strategy	When is the HTML Generated?	Best Use Cases
SSG (Static Site Generation)	At build time	Blogs, landing pages, documentation
SSR (Server-Side Rendering)	On every request	Real-time dashboards, user-specific content
CSR (Client-Side Rendering)	On the client (browser)	Single-page applications (SPAs), interactive UI components

4.2.2 Implementing Server-Side Rendering in Next.js

To enable SSR in Next.js 15, you simply use **async server components** that fetch data dynamically.

Example: Rendering a Server-Side User Profile

tsx

```
// app/profile/page.tsx
async function getUserProfile() {
  const          res          =          await
fetch("https://randomuser.me/api");
  const data = await res.json();
  return data.results[0];
}

export default async function ProfilePage() {
```

```
const user = await getUserProfile();

return (
  <div>
    <h1>User Profile</h1>
    <p><strong>Name:</strong>
{user.name.first} {user.name.last}</p>
    <p><strong>Email:</strong>
{user.email}</p>
    <p><strong>Location:</strong>
{user.location.city},
{user.location.country}</p>
  </div>
);
}
```

How It Works:

- The `getUserProfile()` function fetches user data **at request time**.

- The page is dynamically generated **on every request**.

- Users always see the **latest data** rather than a cached version.

Key Benefits:

Ensures **real-time content** is displayed. Optimized for **SEO**, as search engines receive a fully-rendered page. No need for client-side data fetching.

4.2.3 Using Dynamic Route Parameters with SSR

SSR is powerful when working with **dynamic routes**, such as fetching product details or blog posts based on user input.

Example: Rendering Product Details Dynamically

tsx

```tsx
// app/product/[id]/page.tsx
async function getProduct(id: string) {
  const        res        =        await
fetch(`https://fakestoreapi.com/products/${id
}`);
  return res.json();
}

export default async function ProductPage({
params }: { params: { id: string } }) {
  const product = await getProduct(params.id);

  return (
    <div>
      <h1>{product.title}</h1>
      <p>{product.description}</p>
      <p><strong>Price:</strong>
${product.price}</p>
    </div>
  );
}
```

How It Works:

- The `getProduct(id)` function fetches the product **each time the page is requested**.

83

- The `params.id` value dynamically determines which product to retrieve.
- The product details page **always reflects the latest product information**.

This approach is ideal for:

- E-commerce stores displaying **up-to-date inventory**.
- News websites serving **real-time articles**.
- Dashboards requiring **live data updates**.

4.2.4 Handling API Calls with Caching in SSR

Since SSR runs **on every request**, excessive API calls can slow down performance. Next.js 15 allows **response caching** to improve efficiency.

Example: Enabling Response Caching

tsx

```tsx
// app/weather/page.tsx
async function getWeather() {
  const res = await
fetch("https://api.weatherapi.com/v1/current.
json?key=YOUR_API_KEY&q=London", {
    next: { revalidate: 300 }, // Cache for 5
minutes
  });
  return res.json();
}

export default async function WeatherPage() {
```

```
  const weather = await getWeather();

  return (
    <div>
      <h1>Weather                          in
{weather.location.name}</h1>
      <p><strong>Temperature:</strong>
{weather.current.temp_c}°C</p>
      <p><strong>Condition:</strong>
{weather.current.condition.text}</p>
    </div>
  );
}
```

How It Works:

- The `fetch` call includes `{ next: { revalidate: 300 } }`, caching the response for **5 minutes**.
- Requests within this time frame **use cached data**, reducing API load.
- After 5 minutes, Next.js **fetches fresh data automatically**.

This caching mechanism optimizes performance while maintaining real-time updates where necessary.

4.2.5 When to Use Server-Side Rendering

SSR   is   the   best   choice   for:
Real-time data applications, such as stock market dashboards.

User-specific pages, where content is personalized for logged-in users. **SEO-driven pages** that must always show fresh content.

Avoid SSR if:

Performance is a primary concern (SSG is faster for static content). The page rarely changes (SSG with ISR is more efficient). Large amounts of real-time data need to be displayed frequently (use WebSockets instead).

4.3 Incremental Static Regeneration (ISR)

Incremental Static Regeneration (ISR) is a **hybrid rendering** technique in Next.js that allows pages to be **statically generated at build time but updated incrementally** without requiring a full rebuild. This provides the benefits of **Static Site Generation (SSG)** while allowing updates to be made dynamically.

ISR is particularly useful when:

- Content **changes periodically** but does not require real-time updates.

- Pre-rendering everything at build time is **not practical** due to large amounts of data.

- SEO is important, but **server-side rendering (SSR) is too expensive** in terms of performance.

By using ISR, Next.js regenerates a static page **in the background** at predefined intervals. Users **always see a cached version**, and a fresh version is prepared for future requests without affecting the site's performance.

4.3.1 How ISR Works

ISR introduces a concept called **revalidation**, which defines how frequently a static page should be updated. The process follows these steps:

1. A user requests a page that was **previously generated at build time**.
2. The cached version is **served immediately** for fast performance.
3. Meanwhile, Next.js **regenerates the page in the background**.
4. Once regeneration is complete, the **next user gets the updated version**.

This allows for **efficient updates** without requiring **a full site rebuild**.

ISR vs. Other Rendering Strategies

Rendering Strategy	HTML Generated	Updates When Data Changes?	Best Use Cases
SSG (Static Site Generation)	At build time	No	Blogs, marketing pages
ISR (Incremental Static Regeneration)	At build time, then updated in background	Yes, periodically	News websites, e-commerce product listings

SSR (Server-Side Rendering)	On every request	Yes, immediately	Real-time dashboards, user-specific content

---

4.3.2 Implementing ISR in Next.js

To enable ISR, use the `revalidate` property in your fetch request. This defines the time (in seconds) after which the page should regenerate.

Example: Using ISR for a Blog Page

tsx

```tsx
// app/blog/page.tsx
async function getBlogPosts() {
  const res = await fetch("https://jsonplaceholder.typicode.com/posts", {
    next: { revalidate: 60 }, // Regenerate the page every 60 seconds
  });
  return res.json();
}

export default async function BlogPage() {
  const posts = await getBlogPosts();

  return (
    <div>
      <h1>Latest Blog Posts</h1>
      <ul>
        {posts.slice(0, 5).map((post) => (
```

```
        <li key={post.id}>
          <h2>{post.title}</h2>
          <p>{post.body}</p>
        </li>
      ))}
    </ul>
  </div>
  );
}
```

How It Works:

- The page is **statically generated** at build time.
- The `revalidate: 60` property tells Next.js to **update the page every 60 seconds**.
- The first request serves the **cached page instantly**.
- If a new request arrives after 60 seconds, Next.js regenerates the page **in the background** while still serving the cached version to users.

4.3.3 Using ISR with Dynamic Routes

ISR can be used with **dynamic routes** to fetch and regenerate individual pages as needed.

Example: Using ISR for Product Pages

tsx

```
// app/products/[id]/page.tsx
async function getProduct(id: string) {
```

```
  const          res          =          await
fetch(`https://fakestoreapi.com/products/${id
}`, {
    next: { revalidate: 300 }, // Regenerate
every 5 minutes
  });
  return res.json();
}

export default async function ProductPage({
params }: { params: { id: string } }) {
  const product = await getProduct(params.id);

  return (
    <div>
      <h1>{product.title}</h1>
      <p>{product.description}</p>
      <p><strong>Price:</strong>
${product.price}</p>
    </div>
  );
}
```

Key Features:

- Each product page is **generated on demand** and cached.
- The `revalidate: 300` ensures the page updates **every 5 minutes**.
- **No unnecessary API calls**, improving performance and scalability.

This approach works well for: E-commerce product pages. News articles that update periodically. User-generated content that changes infrequently.

4.3.4 Handling Data Updates with ISR

One challenge of ISR is handling **frequent content updates** without unnecessary re-fetching. By leveraging Next.js caching mechanisms, ISR can be optimized efficiently.

Example: Setting a Short Revalidation Time for Breaking News

tsx

```tsx
// app/news/page.tsx
async function getLatestNews() {
  const res = await fetch("https://api.example.com/news", {
    next: { revalidate: 10 }, // Regenerate every 10 seconds
  });
  return res.json();
}

export default async function NewsPage() {
  const news = await getLatestNews();

  return (
    <div>
      <h1>Breaking News</h1>
      <ul>
        {news.map((article) => (
```

```
      <li key={article.id}>
        <h2>{article.title}</h2>
        <p>{article.summary}</p>
      </li>
    ))}
  </ul>
</div>
);
}
```

Here, the news page:

- **Regenerates every 10 seconds** to reflect recent updates.
- Serves a **cached version** instantly while fetching fresh data in the background.
- Provides an efficient way to handle **frequently changing content** without excessive API requests.

4.3.5 When to Use Incremental Static Regeneration

ISR is the best choice when: **Content updates periodically** but does not need real-time accuracy. **SEO is important**, and pages should be pre-rendered for search engines. The dataset is **too large for full static generation**.

Avoid ISR if:

The page requires **real-time accuracy** (use SSR instead). Content does not change often (use standard SSG). User-specific data is required (use API routes or SSR).

4.4 Hybrid Rendering and When to Use Each

Modern web applications often require a balance between **performance, scalability, and user experience**. Next.js 15 provides a **hybrid rendering model**, allowing developers to combine multiple rendering techniques to optimize different parts of an application.

Hybrid rendering means using **Static Site Generation (SSG), Server-Side Rendering (SSR), Incremental Static Regeneration (ISR), and Client-Side Rendering (CSR)** within the same application based on specific needs. This flexibility ensures that web applications can be both **fast and dynamic**, depending on the content requirements.

4.4.1 Understanding the Different Rendering Strategies

Before diving into hybrid rendering, it is essential to understand the **four main rendering strategies** in Next.js:

1. Static Site Generation (SSG)

How it works:

- Pages are pre-rendered **at build time**.
- HTML and assets are stored in the **CDN for instant delivery**.
- Ideal for pages with **unchanging or rarely updated content**.

Example:

tsx
```
export async function generateStaticParams() {
  const        res        =        await
fetch("https://jsonplaceholder.typicode.com/p
osts");
  const posts = await res.json();
```

```
  return posts.map((post: any) => ({
    id: post.id.toString(),
  }));
}

export default async function BlogPost({
params }: { params: { id: string } }) {
  const res = await fetch(

`https://jsonplaceholder.typicode.com/posts/$
{params.id}`
  );
  const post = await res.json();

  return (
    <div>
      <h1>{post.title}</h1>
      <p>{post.body}</p>
    </div>
  );
}
```

Use SSG when:

- The content does not change frequently.
- Pages need to load **instantly** (e.g., marketing pages, documentation).
- **SEO is important**, and pre-rendered HTML benefits search engines.

2. Server-Side Rendering (SSR)

How it works:

- Pages are generated **on each request**.
- Ensures data is **always fresh**, but increases response time.
- Suitable for content that **changes dynamically per request**.

Example:

tsx
```tsx
export default async function ServerSidePage()
{
  const        res         =        await
fetch("https://jsonplaceholder.typicode.com/p
osts/1", {
    cache: "no-store", // Ensures the request
is made on each request
  });
  const post = await res.json();

  return (
    <div>
      <h1>{post.title}</h1>
      <p>{post.body}</p>
    </div>
  );
}
```

Use SSR when:

- Data needs to be **fetched and updated on every request** (e.g., real-time dashboards, user authentication pages).

- Personalized content must be rendered per **individual user**.

---

3. Incremental Static Regeneration (ISR)

How it works:

- Pages are **statically generated** but **updated periodically**.
- Improves performance while ensuring content freshness.
- Ideal for pages that require **semi-dynamic updates**.

Example:

tsx
```
export default async function ISRPage() {
  const          res          =          await
fetch("https://jsonplaceholder.typicode.com/p
osts/1", {
    next: { revalidate: 60 }, // Regenerates
every 60 seconds
  });
  const post = await res.json();

  return (
    <div>
      <h1>{post.title}</h1>
      <p>{post.body}</p>
    </div>
  );
```

```
}
```

Use ISR when:

- Pages need periodic updates **without full rebuilds**.

- The application must balance **performance and fresh content** (e.g., news sites, product listings).

---

4. Client-Side Rendering (CSR)

How it works:

- The page is rendered in the **browser after loading**.
- Often used with frameworks like **React Query or SWR** for fetching data.
- Great for highly **interactive and user-specific content**.

Example:

tsx
```tsx
"use client";

import { useEffect, useState } from "react";

export default function CSRPage() {
  const [post, setPost] = useState(null);

  useEffect(() => {
```

```
fetch("https://jsonplaceholder.typicode.com/p
osts/1")
      .then((res) => res.json())
      .then((data) => setPost(data));
  }, []);

  if (!post) return <p>Loading...</p>;

  return (
    <div>
      <h1>{post.title}</h1>
      <p>{post.body}</p>
    </div>
  );
}
```

Use CSR when:

- The data is **user-specific and not SEO-critical**.
- Content updates in **real-time** (e.g., chat applications, dashboards).

4.4.2 Implementing Hybrid Rendering

A **hybrid approach** combines multiple rendering strategies to **optimize performance and usability**.

Example: Using Hybrid Rendering in an E-commerce Application

Consider an e-commerce site where:

98

- The homepage is **statically generated** (SSG) for fast loading.
- Product pages use **ISR** to update periodically.
- The cart uses **CSR** since it is user-specific.
- The checkout process is **SSR** to ensure fresh order details.

Folder structure:

css

```
app/
 ├── page.tsx (SSG - Homepage)
 ├── products/
 │    ├── page.tsx (ISR - Product listing)
 │    ├── [id]/
 │         ├── page.tsx (ISR - Product details)
 ├── cart/
 │    ├── page.tsx (CSR - Client-rendered cart)
 ├── checkout/
 │    ├── page.tsx (SSR - Secure checkout)
```

Example Code for Each Page

1. Homepage (SSG)

tsx

```tsx
export default function HomePage() {
  return <h1>Welcome to Our Store</h1>;
}
```

2. Product Listing (ISR)

tsx

```tsx
export default async function
ProductListPage() {
  const res = await
fetch("https://fakestoreapi.com/products", {
    next: { revalidate: 300 },
  });
  const products = await res.json();

  return (
    <ul>
      {products.map((product) => (
        <li
key={product.id}>{product.title}</li>
      ))}
    </ul>
  );
}
```

3. Cart (CSR)

tsx

```tsx
"use client";
import { useState } from "react";
export default function CartPage() {
  const [cart, setCart] = useState([]);
  return <h1>Shopping Cart ({cart.length}
items)</h1>;
}
```

4. Checkout (SSR)

tsx
```tsx
export default async function CheckoutPage() {
  const         res        =        await
fetch("https://api.example.com/orders", {
    cache: "no-store",
  });
  const order = await res.json();

  return <h1>Checkout Order #{order.id}</h1>;
}
```

4.4.3 Choosing the Right Rendering Strategy

Scenario	Recommended Rendering
Static content (marketing pages, blogs)	**SSG**
Frequently updated but not real-time (news, product listings)	**ISR**
User-specific data (profile pages, dashboards)	**CSR**
Highly dynamic and real-time (authentication, checkout)	**SSR**

Chapter 5: Fetching Data in Next.js

Fetching data efficiently is a crucial aspect of modern web development. Next.js 15 offers multiple strategies for data fetching, including **static data fetching, server-side fetching, and client-side fetching**. Each method has specific use cases that balance **performance, scalability, and freshness**.

This chapter covers the primary data-fetching mechanisms in Next.js:

- **Static Data Fetching** with `getStaticProps` (SSG)
- **Server-Side Data Fetching** with `getServerSideProps` (SSR)
- **Client-Side Fetching** with SWR
- **API Routes and Fetching from External Sources**

By the end of this chapter, you will understand when and how to use each approach effectively.

5.1 Using getStaticProps for Static Data Fetching

Static Site Generation (SSG) is one of the most powerful features of Next.js, enabling developers to pre-render pages at build time. This approach ensures that web pages load **instantly**, improving **performance, SEO, and scalability**. Next.js achieves this using `getStaticProps`, a function that allows data to be **fetched ahead of time** and embedded directly into the generated HTML files.

In this section, you will learn:

- **How** `getStaticProps` **works** and when to use it.

- **The advantages and limitations** of static data fetching.
- **A hands-on example** that fetches and pre-renders content from an external API.

5.1.1 Understanding `getStaticProps`

What is `getStaticProps`?

`getStaticProps` is a **special Next.js function** that runs at **build time**. It allows Next.js to fetch data **before serving the page**, ensuring that the content is pre-rendered into a **static HTML file**.

Unlike traditional client-side data fetching, where data is fetched **on every page load**, `getStaticProps` fetches data **once during build time**. This means:

- The page loads **instantly**, as no additional requests are required.
- The **data is cached and served via a CDN**, making it extremely fast.
- The content **remains static until the next build or revalidation**.

5.1.2 When to Use `getStaticProps`

`getStaticProps` is ideal for pages where:

- **Data does not change frequently**, such as blogs, marketing pages, and documentation.

- **SEO is important**, since pages are fully rendered before being indexed.
- **Performance is a priority**, as static pages load much faster than dynamically rendered ones.

Examples of Use Cases

- A **blog** displaying articles fetched from a CMS.
- A **product catalog** that rarely updates.
- A **landing page** with fixed content that does not require frequent updates.

However, getStaticProps **should not** be used when:

- The content **changes frequently** and needs to be updated dynamically.
- The page needs **personalized or user-specific data**.
- The data must be fetched **on every request** (use getServerSideProps instead).

5.1.3 Implementing getStaticProps

Example: Fetching and Pre-Rendering Blog Posts

In this example, we will create a **static blog page** that fetches a list of posts from an external API using getStaticProps.

Steps:

1. Use getStaticProps to fetch blog posts during build time.

2. Pass the fetched data as props to the page component.

3. Render the data in a static HTML page.

Code Implementation

`pages/blog.js` – **A Static Blog Page**

tsx
```tsx
export async function getStaticProps() {
  // Fetch data from an external API
  const          res          =          await
fetch("https://jsonplaceholder.typicode.com/p
osts");
  const posts = await res.json();

  return {
    props: { posts }, // Pass the fetched data
as props
  };
}

export default function BlogPage({ posts }) {
  return (
    <div>
      <h1>Blog Posts</h1>
      <ul>
        {posts.map((post) => (
          <li key={post.id}>{post.title}</li>
        ))}
      </ul>
    </div>
  );
```

```
}
```

Code Breakdown

1. **Fetching Data at Build Time:**

   o   The `fetch` function retrieves data from an API.

   o   The response is converted into JSON format.

   o   The fetched data is returned inside `props`.

2. **Pre-Rendering the Page:**

   o   The `BlogPage` component receives the fetched `posts` as props.

   o   The data is rendered **statically**, meaning the page will not change unless a rebuild occurs.

5.1.4 Enhancing Static Generation with `getStaticPaths`

Sometimes, static generation requires **dynamic paths**, such as **individual blog posts**. Next.js provides `getStaticPaths` to **pre-generate pages for dynamic routes**.

Example: Pre-Generating Individual Blog Posts

If we want to **pre-render individual blog post pages**, we need both `getStaticProps` and `getStaticPaths`.

pages/blog/[id].js – A Static Blog Post Page

tsx

```tsx
export async function getStaticPaths() {
  const         res         =         await
fetch("https://jsonplaceholder.typicode.com/p
osts");
  const posts = await res.json();

  // Generate paths for each post
  const paths = posts.map((post) => ({
    params: { id: post.id.toString() },
  }));

  return { paths, fallback: false };
}

export async function getStaticProps({ params
}) {
  const res = await fetch(

`https://jsonplaceholder.typicode.com/posts/$
{params.id}`
  );
  const post = await res.json();

  return {
    props: { post },
  };
}

export default function PostPage({ post }) {
```

```tsx
  return (
    <div>
      <h1>{post.title}</h1>
      <p>{post.body}</p>
    </div>
  );
}
```

How It Works

1. `getStaticPaths` **fetches all posts** and generates an array of `paths`.
2. **Next.js pre-builds these pages** based on the available post IDs.
3. `getStaticProps` **fetches data for each individual post and pre-renders it.**

5.1.5 Handling Revalidation with Incremental Static Regeneration (ISR)

By default, `getStaticProps` **only runs at build time**, meaning the content remains the same until the next deployment. However, Next.js **supports Incremental Static Regeneration (ISR)**, allowing static pages to be **updated without a full rebuild.**

Example: Revalidating Data Every 60 Seconds

tsx

```tsx
export async function getStaticProps() {
  const       res       =       await
fetch("https://jsonplaceholder.typicode.com/p
osts");
```

```
  const posts = await res.json();

  return {
    props: { posts },
    revalidate: 60, // Rebuilds the page every
60 seconds
  };
}
```

Key Benefits of ISR

- **Combines the speed of static generation** with the flexibility of real-time updates.

- **Only rebuilds pages when necessary**, reducing server load.

- Ensures that **users always see fresh content** without waiting for a full deployment.

5.2 Using getServerSideProps for Server-Side Data Fetching

While getStaticProps enables **pre-rendering at build time**, there are many scenarios where data must be fetched **on every request**. This is where getServerSideProps comes in. It allows Next.js to fetch data **on the server for each request**, ensuring that users always see the most up-to-date content.

5.2.1 Understanding `getServerSideProps`

What is `getServerSideProps`?

`getServerSideProps` is a special function in Next.js that runs **on the server for every request**. Unlike `getStaticProps`, which fetches data **once during build time**, `getServerSideProps`:

- **Executes on every request**, ensuring that data is always fresh.

- **Runs only on the server**, meaning the client does not see API keys or sensitive logic.

- **Returns props to the page**, allowing Next.js to pre-render it dynamically.

This makes it ideal for scenarios where **data changes frequently** or **needs to be personalized per request**.

5.2.2 When to Use `getServerSideProps`

Use `getServerSideProps` when:

- **Data must be updated on every request**, such as stock prices, news feeds, or user dashboards.
- **Personalized content is required**, such as user profiles or session-based data.
- **SEO is important**, and the content needs to be indexed by search engines.

- **Authentication is needed**, where requests must be validated on the server.

Examples of Use Cases

- A **real-time dashboard** displaying live statistics.
- A **personalized user profile page** that requires authentication.
- A **search results page** that depends on user input.

However, `getServerSideProps` **should not** be used when:

- The data is **static** and does not need to change frequently.
- Performance is a priority, as it **introduces a server request for every page load**.
- The page must be **cached and served quickly**.

5.2.3 Implementing `getServerSideProps`

Example: Fetching Dynamic User Data

In this example, we will create a **user profile page** that fetches user data from an API **on each request**.

Steps:

1. Use `getServerSideProps` to fetch user data on each request.
2. Pass the fetched data as props to the page component.
3. Render the user data dynamically.

Code Implementation

`pages/profile.js` – A Server-Rendered User Profile Page

tsx

```
export async function getServerSideProps() {
  // Fetch data from an external API
  const          res          =          await
fetch("https://jsonplaceholder.typicode.com/u
sers/1");
  const user = await res.json();

  return {
    props: { user }, // Pass the fetched data
as props
  };
}


export default function ProfilePage({ user })
{
  return (
    <div>
      <h1>User Profile</h1>
      <p><strong>Name:</strong>
{user.name}</p>
      <p><strong>Email:</strong>
{user.email}</p>
      <p><strong>Website:</strong>
{user.website}</p>
    </div>
  );
}
```

Code Breakdown

1. **Fetching Data on Every Request:**

   - `fetch` retrieves the latest user data from an API.

   - The response is converted into JSON format.

   - The fetched data is returned inside `props`.

2. **Rendering the Page Dynamically:**

   - The `ProfilePage` component receives the `user` data as props.

   - The page is re-rendered on **every request**, ensuring that the data is always up to date.

5.2.4 Handling Query Parameters with `getServerSideProps`

Many applications require **query parameters** to fetch specific data dynamically. `getServerSideProps` receives a `context` object that includes the request parameters, which can be used to modify the fetched data.

Example: Fetching User Data Dynamically Based on Query Parameters

This example demonstrates how to fetch a **specific user profile** dynamically using query parameters.

`pages/profile/[id].js` – **Dynamic User Profiles**

tsx

```tsx
export async function getServerSideProps({
params }) {
  const res = await
fetch(`https://jsonplaceholder.typicode.com/u
sers/${params.id}`);
  const user = await res.json();

  return {
    props: { user },
  };
}

export default function ProfilePage({ user })
{
  return (
    <div>
      <h1>{user.name}'s Profile</h1>
      <p><strong>Email:</strong>
{user.email}</p>
      <p><strong>Website:</strong>
{user.website}</p>
    </div>
  );
}
```

How It Works

1. **Extracting Query Parameters:**

114

- `params.id` is obtained from the URL
  (`/profile/1` → `id = 1`).

- The API fetches user data based on the extracted `id`.

2. **Dynamic Pre-Rendering:**
   - Every request generates a fresh page with updated data.
   - The correct user profile is displayed based on the URL.

5.2.5 Comparing `getStaticProps` and `getServerSideProps`

Both functions **pre-render pages**, but they serve different purposes.

Feature	`getStaticProps`	`getServerSideProps`
Runs at build time	Yes	No
Runs on every request	No	Yes
Best for	Static content, SEO	Dynamic content, real-time data
Performance	Fast (cached static pages)	Slower (server-side fetching)
Personalized data	No	Yes
Use cases	Blogs, documentation	Dashboards, user profiles, search

5.2.6 Performance Considerations

Since `getServerSideProps` fetches data **on every request**, it **can impact performance** if not optimized.

Best Practices for Optimizing `getServerSideProps`

1. **Reduce API response time** by using optimized queries and caching strategies.

2. **Minimize unnecessary requests** by avoiding re-fetching static data.

3. **Use server-side caching** with tools like Redis or database optimizations.

4. **Optimize backend performance** to handle frequent requests efficiently.

5.3 Client-Side Fetching with SWR

While **server-side rendering (SSR)** ensures data is fetched before rendering, there are cases where fetching data on the client side is more efficient. Client-side fetching is useful for **real-time updates, interactive components, and dynamic data that doesn't require SEO optimization**.

In Next.js, **SWR (Stale-While-Revalidate)** is a powerful library for client-side data fetching. It improves performance by **fetching, caching, and automatically updating data** in the background.

116

5.3.1 Understanding SWR

What is SWR?

SWR is a **lightweight data-fetching library** built by the Vercel team (creators of Next.js). It follows the **Stale-While-Revalidate** strategy:

1. **Returns cached data instantly** (stale data).

2. **Fetches fresh data in the background** to update the cache.

3. **Re-renders the component** when fresh data arrives.

This makes SWR a great choice for:

- **Fetching frequently updated data** (e.g., live dashboards, notifications, real-time comments).

- **Improving user experience** by showing cached content before fetching new data.

- **Reducing unnecessary API calls** by caching and revalidating data only when needed.

5.3.2 Installing SWR

Before using SWR, install the library in your Next.js project:

sh

```
npm install swr
```

or

sh

```
yarn add swr
```

Once installed, SWR can be used to fetch and manage client-side data.

5.3.3 Using SWR for Client-Side Data Fetching

Basic Example: Fetching Data from an API

The useSWR hook is the core of SWR. It takes two main arguments:

1. **A key (usually the API URL)** – used to identify and cache the request.

2. **A fetcher function** – a function that retrieves the data.

tsx

```tsx
import useSWR from "swr";

// Fetcher function that retrieves data from
an API
const fetcher = (url) => fetch(url).then((res)
=> res.json());

export default function Users() {
  // Use SWR to fetch data from an API
```

```
  const { data, error, isLoading } = useSWR(

"https://jsonplaceholder.typicode.com/users",
    fetcher
  );

  if (isLoading) return <p>Loading...</p>;
  if   (error)   return   <p>Error   loading
users.</p>;

  return (
    <div>
      <h1>Users</h1>
      <ul>
        {data.map((user) => (
          <li    key={user.id}>{user.name}   -
{user.email}</li>
        ))}
      </ul>
    </div>
  );
}
```

5.3.4 Understanding the Code

1. **The fetcher function:**

   o `fetch(url).then((res) => res.json())`
     retrieves data and converts it to JSON.

- This function can be customized to use authentication headers or other configurations.

2. **Using `useSWR`:**

- `useSWR("API_URL", fetcher)` fetches data from the given API.
- It automatically caches the response and updates it in the background.

3. **Handling loading and errors:**

- `isLoading` ensures the page displays a loading message until data arrives.
- `error` handles errors gracefully if the request fails.

5.3.5 Handling Automatic Revalidation

SWR automatically **revalidates data** when:

- The **user revisits the page** (tab focus).
- The **window regains focus** after being inactive.
- The **network reconnects** after being offline.

This behavior improves performance while keeping data fresh.

To customize revalidation behavior, pass configuration options:

tsx
```
const { data, error } = useSWR(
```

```
  "https://jsonplaceholder.typicode.com/users",
  fetcher,
  {
    refreshInterval: 5000, // Re-fetch data
every 5 seconds
    revalidateOnFocus: false, // Disable re-
fetching when tab gains focus
  }
);
```

5.3.6 Optimizing Performance with SWR

1. Fetching Data Conditionally

Sometimes, fetching data should depend on a specific condition (e.g., a user being logged in). SWR allows conditional fetching:

tsx
```
const { data, error } = useSWR(userId ?
`/api/user/${userId}` : null, fetcher);
```

If userId is null, SWR does not fetch data.

2. Mutating Data Manually

Instead of waiting for SWR to revalidate, you can **manually update cached data** using mutate:

tsx
```
import useSWR, { mutate } from "swr";
const { data } = useSWR("/api/user", fetcher);
// Manually update cached data
const updateUser = async () => {
```

121

```
  await fetch("/api/update-user", { method:
"POST" });
  mutate("/api/user"); // Re-fetch data
};
```

3. Error Handling and Retry Strategy

SWR automatically retries failed requests, but you can customize retry behavior:

tsx
```
const { data, error } = useSWR("/api/user",
fetcher, {
  shouldRetryOnError:   false,   //   Disable
automatic retries
  errorRetryInterval: 3000, // Retry every 3
seconds if an error occurs
});
```

5.3.7 Comparing SWR and getServerSideProps

Feature	SWR (Client-Side)	getServerSide Props (Server-Side)
Executes on	Client	Server
Best for	Dynamic UI updates, real-time data	SEO, pre-rendered content
Performance	Faster after first load	Slower (fetches on each request)

Data freshness	Updates automatically	Stays static until next request
Caching	Yes, client-side	No, fetches every request

When to Use SWR

- Fetching real-time or frequently changing data.
- Reducing server load by caching responses.
- Fetching user-specific data that doesn't need SEO.

When to Use getServerSideProps

- Fetching sensitive data on the server.
- Ensuring data is available before rendering.
- Handling SEO-critical content.

5.4 API Routes and Fetching from External Sources

Next.js provides a built-in API route system that allows developers to create backend functionality within a Next.js application. API routes are particularly useful for handling requests, processing data, and serving external APIs without requiring a separate backend server.

5.4.1 Understanding API Routes in Next.js

What Are API Routes?

API routes in Next.js enable developers to define **server-side endpoints** directly within the project. These endpoints:

- Run on the **server** instead of the client.
- Can handle **GET, POST, PUT, DELETE**, and other HTTP methods.
- Do not require an external backend (such as Express.js) to handle requests.

API routes are defined inside the `pages/api/` directory. Each file inside this folder automatically becomes an API endpoint that can be accessed via an HTTP request.

Basic Example: Creating an API Route

Create a new file inside `pages/api/hello.js`:

javascript

```
// pages/api/hello.js

export default function handler(req, res) {
  res.status(200).json({ message: "Hello from
Next.js API" });
}
```

Now, if you visit `http://localhost:3000/api/hello` in your browser, you will see:

json
```
{
  "message": "Hello from Next.js API"
}
```

5.4.2 Handling Different HTTP Methods

API routes can process different types of requests, such as **GET, POST, PUT, DELETE**. Use `req.method` to handle different cases.

Example: Handling Multiple HTTP Methods

javascript

```javascript
// pages/api/user.js

export default function handler(req, res) {
  if (req.method === "GET") {
    res.status(200).json({ user: "John Doe",
email: "john@example.com" });
  } else if (req.method === "POST") {
    res.status(201).json({  message:  "User
created successfully" });
  } else {
    res.status(405).json({ error: "Method Not
Allowed" });
  }
}
```

- `GET /api/user` returns a user object.
- `POST /api/user` simulates creating a user.
- Other methods receive a `405 Method Not Allowed` response.

5.4.3 Fetching External Data from an API

Next.js API routes can also serve as **middleware** to fetch data from external sources and return it to the frontend.

Example: Fetching Data from an External API

Let's create an API route that fetches a list of users from an external API (`jsonplaceholder.typicode.com`).

javascript

```javascript
// pages/api/users.js

export default async function handler(req, res) {
  try {
    const response = await fetch("https://jsonplaceholder.typicode.com/users");
    const data = await response.json();
    res.status(200).json(data);
  } catch (error) {
    res.status(500).json({ error: "Failed to fetch users" });
  }
}
```

Now, when visiting `http://localhost:3000/api/users`, the API route will:

1. Fetch users from the external API.

2. Return the JSON response.

3. Handle errors with a `500 Internal Server Error` if the request fails.

5.4.4 Fetching API Route Data from the Frontend

To consume this API route in a Next.js page, use the **fetch API** or useSWR for client-side fetching.

Example: Fetching API Route Data on the Client

tsx

```tsx
import useSWR from "swr";

// Fetcher function
const fetcher = (url) => fetch(url).then((res)
=> res.json());

export default function UsersPage() {
  const { data, error, isLoading } =
useSWR("/api/users", fetcher);

  if (isLoading) return <p>Loading...</p>;
  if (error) return <p>Error loading
users.</p>;

  return (
    <div>
      <h1>Users</h1>
      <ul>
        {data.map((user) => (
          <li key={user.id}>{user.name} -
{user.email}</li>
        ))}
      </ul>
```

```
    </div>
  );
}
```

This approach:

- Uses the `/api/users` route to fetch data.

- Caches and revalidates data automatically with SWR.

- Handles loading and error states gracefully.

5.4.5 Using API Routes with Server-Side Rendering

Next.js API routes can also be consumed using **server-side rendering (SSR)** with `getServerSideProps`.

Example: Fetching API Data with SSR

tsx

```
export async function getServerSideProps() {
  const          res          =          await
fetch("http://localhost:3000/api/users");
  const users = await res.json();

  return { props: { users } };
}

export default function UsersPage({ users }) {
  return (
```

```
  <div>
    <h1>Users</h1>
    <ul>
      {users.map((user) => (
        <li   key={user.id}>{user.name}   -
{user.email}</li>
      ))}
    </ul>
  </div>
  );
}
```

Here, getServerSideProps fetches data on **each request**, ensuring fresh data every time the page loads.

5.4.6 API Route Best Practices

To ensure efficient and scalable API development in Next.js, follow these best practices:

Use   Middleware   for   Authentication
Protect   API   routes   using   authentication   middleware.

javascript

```
import { verifyToken } from "../../lib/auth";
// Custom authentication function

export default function handler(req, res) {
  if (!verifyToken(req)) {
```

```
    return    res.status(401).json({    error:
"Unauthorized" });
  }

  res.status(200).json({              message:
"Authenticated request" });
}
```

1. **Handle Errors Gracefully**
   Always wrap external API calls in `try/catch` blocks to
   prevent application crashes.

2. **Optimize Performance with Caching**
   Implement caching mechanisms (e.g., Redis, SWR) to reduce
   API load.

3. **Validate Request Data**
   Use libraries like `joi` or `zod` to validate incoming request data.

4. **Follow RESTful and API Design Principles**
   Use consistent endpoints, HTTP methods, and meaningful
   status codes.

Chapter 6: Building APIs with Next.js

APIs (Application Programming Interfaces) are essential for modern web applications, enabling communication between the frontend and backend. Next.js provides built-in API routes, allowing developers to create scalable, efficient APIs without needing an external backend framework like Express.

This chapter will cover:

- How to create API routes in Next.js.
- Handling API requests using both REST and GraphQL.
- Connecting Next.js APIs to databases like PostgreSQL, MongoDB, and Firebase.
- Securing API endpoints with authentication and middleware.

By the end of this chapter, you will be able to build full-featured APIs using Next.js, integrate them with databases, and implement authentication and security best practices.

6.1 Creating API Routes in Next.js

Next.js provides a built-in way to create API routes, allowing developers to define backend functionality within the same project as their frontend. Unlike traditional full-stack applications that require a separate backend framework like Express, Next.js API routes operate as serverless functions, executing only when called.

By the end of this section, you will be able to build efficient API endpoints that can be used to communicate with a frontend application, fetch data from databases, or integrate with third-party services.

6.1.1 Understanding API Routes in Next.js

What Are API Routes?

API routes in Next.js allow developers to create server-side functions that handle HTTP requests. These routes run on the server and provide a backend layer for your application without requiring a separate API server.

Key benefits of API routes in Next.js:

- **Built-in API handling** – No need for an external backend framework.

- **Server-side execution** – API routes execute only when requested, reducing client-side load.

- **Seamless integration** – Can interact with databases, authentication systems, and external APIs.

- **Automatic API route creation** – Files inside `pages/api/` automatically become API endpoints.

Folder Structure for API Routes

API routes are placed inside the `pages/api/` directory of a Next.js project. Each file in this directory automatically becomes an endpoint that can be accessed via an HTTP request.

Example folder structure:

lua

```
my-nextjs-app/
|-- pages/
|   |-- index.js
|   |-- about.js
|   |-- api/
|   |   |-- hello.js
|   |   |-- users.js
|   |   |-- products.js
|-- public/
|-- styles/
|-- next.config.js
|-- package.json
```

6.1.2 Creating a Basic API Route

Creating an API route in Next.js is straightforward. Every file inside `pages/api/` exports a function that handles HTTP requests and responses.

Example: Hello World API

Create a new file `pages/api/hello.js`:

javascript

```
// pages/api/hello.js
```

133

```
export default function handler(req, res) {
  res.status(200).json({ message: "Hello from
Next.js API" });
}
```

Explanation:

- The function `handler(req, res)` handles incoming HTTP requests.

- `req` (request) contains information about the incoming request (method, headers, body).

- `res` (response) is used to send data back to the client.

- `res.status(200).json({ message: "Hello from Next.js API" })` sends a JSON response with HTTP status `200 OK`.

Testing the API Route

Start your Next.js development server:

bash

```
npm run dev
```

Visit `http://localhost:3000/api/hello` in a browser or API testing tool (like Postman), and you should see the following JSON response:

```json
{
  "message": "Hello from Next.js API"
}
```

6.1.3 Handling HTTP Methods

API routes can handle multiple HTTP methods, such as GET, POST, PUT, and DELETE. This makes them ideal for building RESTful APIs.

Example: Handling Multiple HTTP Methods

Create a new file pages/api/user.js:

javascript
```javascript
// pages/api/user.js

export default function handler(req, res) {
  if (req.method === "GET") {
    res.status(200).json({ user: "John Doe",
email: "john@example.com" });
  } else if (req.method === "POST") {
    const { name, email } = req.body;
    res.status(201).json({   message:   "User
created successfully", user: { name, email }
});
  } else {
    res.status(405).json({ error: "Method Not
Allowed" });
  }
}
```

Explanation:

- If the request method is GET, the API returns a predefined user object.

- If the request method is POST, it extracts name and email from the request body and returns a success message.

- If any other method is used, it returns an error response with HTTP status 405 Method Not Allowed.

Testing the API

GET Request

bash

```
curl -X GET http://localhost:3000/api/user
```

Response:

json

```
{
  "user": "John Doe",
  "email": "john@example.com"
}
```

POST Request

bash

```
curl -X POST http://localhost:3000/api/user -
H   "Content-Type:   application/json"   -d
```

```
'{"name":            "Alice",            "email":
"alice@example.com"}'
```

Response:

json

```json
{
  "message": "User created successfully",
  "user": {
    "name": "Alice",
    "email": "alice@example.com"
  }
}
```

6.1.4 Handling Query Parameters and Dynamic Routes

Next.js allows dynamic API routes where parameters can be passed in the URL.

Example: Dynamic API Route

Create a file `pages/api/user/[id].js`:

javascript

```javascript
// pages/api/user/[id].js

export default function handler(req, res) {
  const { id } = req.query;
```

137

```javascript
if (req.method === "GET") {
    res.status(200).json({ userId: id, name:
`User ${id}` });
  } else {
    res.status(405).json({ error: "Method Not
Allowed" });
  }
}
```

Explanation:

- `req.query` extracts the `id` parameter from the URL.

- If the request method is GET, it returns a user object with the provided `id`.

Testing the API

Visit `http://localhost:3000/api/user/5` in the browser.

Response:

json

```json
{
  "userId": "5",
  "name": "User 5"
}
```

6.1.5 Handling Errors and Validations

Proper error handling ensures a robust API that returns meaningful responses.

Example: Handling Errors

javascript

```javascript
// pages/api/user.js

export default function handler(req, res) {
  try {
    if (req.method !== "POST") {
      throw new Error("Only POST requests are allowed");
    }

    const { name, email } = req.body;
    if (!name || !email) {
      throw new Error("Missing required fields: name and email");
    }

    res.status(201).json({ message: "User created successfully", user: { name, email } });
  } catch (error) {
    res.status(400).json({ error: error.message });
  }
}
```

Explanation:

- Throws an error if the request method is not POST.

- Validates that name and email are provided.

- Catches any errors and returns a 400 Bad Request response.

6.2 Handling Requests with REST and GraphQL

Modern web applications require efficient communication between the frontend and backend. Next.js supports both **REST** and **GraphQL** APIs, allowing developers to choose the best approach for their project.

6.2.1 REST vs. GraphQL: Key Differences

What Is REST?

REST (Representational State Transfer) is a widely used architectural style for designing networked applications. REST APIs use **HTTP methods** to perform CRUD (Create, Read, Update, Delete) operations on resources.

Example HTTP methods used in REST:

- **GET** – Retrieve data.
- **POST** – Create a new resource.
- **PUT/PATCH** – Update an existing resource.
- **DELETE** – Remove a resource.

Advantages of REST:

✓ Simple and widely supported.
✓ Works well with caching mechanisms.
✓ Clear separation of concerns.

Limitations of REST:

✖ Over-fetching or under-fetching of data.
✖ Requires multiple endpoints for different resources.

What Is GraphQL?

GraphQL is a query language for APIs that allows clients to request only the data they need. Instead of multiple endpoints, GraphQL provides a **single endpoint** where clients specify the exact fields they want.

Advantages of GraphQL:

✓ Fetch only the required data, reducing over-fetching.
✓ Strongly typed schema provides better validation.
✓ Ideal for complex relationships between data.

Limitations of GraphQL:

✖ Requires a GraphQL server setup.
✖ More complex to cache compared to REST.

6.2.2 Implementing REST API Endpoints in Next.js

Creating a RESTful API

To build a REST API in Next.js, create API routes inside the `pages/api/` directory. Each file in this directory acts as an endpoint.

Example: CRUD API for Users

Create a new file `pages/api/users.js`:

javascript
```
// pages/api/users.js

const users = [
  { id: 1, name: "Alice", email:
"alice@example.com" },
  { id: 2, name: "Bob", email:
"bob@example.com" },
];

export default function handler(req, res) {
  if (req.method === "GET") {
    res.status(200).json(users);
  } else if (req.method === "POST") {
    const { name, email } = req.body;
    if (!name || !email) {
      return res.status(400).json({ error:
"Missing name or email" });
    }

    const newUser = { id: users.length + 1,
name, email };
```

```
    users.push(newUser);
    res.status(201).json(newUser);
  } else {
    res.status(405).json({ error: "Method Not
Allowed" });
  }
}
```

Explanation:

- **GET** request returns a list of users.
- **POST** request creates a new user and adds it to the `users` array.
- If the request method is not supported, it returns `405 Method Not Allowed`.

Testing the API

GET request:

bash
```
curl -X GET http://localhost:3000/api/users
```

POST request:

bash
```
curl -X POST http://localhost:3000/api/users -
H    "Content-Type:    application/json"    -d
'{"name":        "Charlie",        "email":
"charlie@example.com"}'
```

Response:

json

```json
{
  "id": 3,
  "name": "Charlie",
  "email": "charlie@example.com"
}
```

6.2.3 Implementing a GraphQL API in Next.js

Unlike REST, GraphQL requires a dedicated **GraphQL server** to process queries. In Next.js, we can use **Apollo Server** to create a GraphQL API.

Installing Dependencies

Run the following command to install Apollo Server:

bash
```bash
npm install apollo-server-micro graphql
```

Setting Up a GraphQL API

Create a new file `pages/api/graphql.js`:

javascript
```javascript
// pages/api/graphql.js
import { ApolloServer, gql } from "apollo-server-micro";
```

```javascript
const typeDefs = gql`
  type User {
    id: ID!
    name: String!
    email: String!
  }

  type Query {
    users: [User]
    user(id: ID!): User
  }

  type Mutation {
    addUser(name: String!, email: String!):
User
  }
`;

const users = [
  { id: "1", name: "Alice", email:
"alice@example.com" },
  { id: "2", name: "Bob", email:
"bob@example.com" },
];

const resolvers = {
  Query: {
    users: () => users,
    user: (_, { id }) => users.find(user =>
user.id === id),
  },
```

```
  Mutation: {
    addUser: (_, { name, email }) => {
      const    newUser    =    {    id:
String(users.length + 1), name, email };
      users.push(newUser);
      return newUser;
    },
  },
};

const   apolloServer   =   new   ApolloServer({
typeDefs, resolvers });

export   default   apolloServer.createHandler({
path: "/api/graphql" });

export const config = {
  api: {
    bodyParser: false,
  },
};
```

Explanation:

- Defines a **GraphQL schema (`typeDefs`)** that specifies the shape of the API.
- Implements **query resolvers** to fetch all users or a specific user.
- Implements a **mutation resolver** to add a new user.
- Sets up Apollo Server to handle GraphQL requests.

6.2.4 Querying the GraphQL API

Once the server is running, open GraphQL Playground at:

bash
```
http://localhost:3000/api/graphql
```

Fetch All Users

Query:

graphql

```graphql
query {
  users {
    id
    name
    email
  }
}
```

Response:

json
```json
{
  "data": {
    "users": [
      { "id": "1", "name": "Alice", "email":
"alice@example.com" },
      { "id": "2", "name": "Bob", "email":
"bob@example.com" }
    ]
```

Fetch a User by ID

Query:

```graphql
query {
  user(id: "1") {
    name
    email
  }
}
```

Response:

```json
{
  "data": {
    "user": { "name": "Alice", "email":
"alice@example.com" }
  }
}
```

Add a New User

Mutation:

```graphql
mutation {
```

```
  addUser(name:        "Charlie",        email:
"charlie@example.com") {
    id
    name
    email
  }
}
```

Response:

json

```json
{
  "data": {
    "addUser": {
      "id": "3",
      "name": "Charlie",
      "email": "charlie@example.com"
    }
  }
}
```

6.3 Connecting to Databases (PostgreSQL, MongoDB, Firebase)

A full-stack Next.js application requires persistent data storage. Choosing the right database depends on factors like scalability, structure, and query flexibility. In this section, we will cover:

- How to connect a Next.js API to **PostgreSQL**, **MongoDB**, and **Firebase**.

- Setting up database connections using best practices.

- Performing CRUD operations for real-world applications.

By the end of this section, you will be able to integrate Next.js APIs with different databases, ensuring secure and efficient data handling.

6.3.1 Using PostgreSQL with Next.js

Why Use PostgreSQL?

PostgreSQL is a **relational database** known for its reliability, extensibility, and performance. It is ideal for structured data, complex queries, and transactional consistency.

Installing PostgreSQL and Prisma

We will use **Prisma ORM** to simplify database interactions in Next.js. Install the required dependencies:

bash

```
npm install @prisma/client
npm install --save-dev prisma
```

Initialize Prisma:

bash

```
npx prisma init
```

This creates a `prisma/schema.prisma` file where you define your database schema.

Configuring PostgreSQL Connection

Modify the `.env` file:

env

```
DATABASE_URL="postgresql://user:password@loca
lhost:5432/mydatabase"
```

Define a **User model** in `prisma/schema.prisma`:

prisma

```
model User {
  id    Int    @id @default(autoincrement())
  name  String
  email String  @unique
}
```

Apply the schema:

bash
```
npx prisma migrate dev --name init
```

Creating an API Route for Users

Create a new file `pages/api/users.js`:

javascript
```javascript
import { PrismaClient } from "@prisma/client";
const prisma = new PrismaClient();
export default async function handler(req,
res) {
  if (req.method === "GET") {
    const       users       =       await
prisma.user.findMany();
    res.status(200).json(users);
  } else if (req.method === "POST") {
    const { name, email } = req.body;
    if (!name || !email) {
      return  res.status(400).json({  error:
"Name and email are required" });
    }

    const newUser = await prisma.user.create({
      data: { name, email },
    });
    res.status(201).json(newUser);
  } else {
    res.status(405).json({ error: "Method Not
Allowed" });
  }
}
```

Testing the API

GET request:

bash

```
curl -X GET http://localhost:3000/api/users
```

POST request:

bash
```
curl -X POST http://localhost:3000/api/users -
H    "Content-Type:    application/json"    -d
'{"name":           "Alice",           "email":
"alice@example.com"}'
```

PostgreSQL is now integrated with Next.js using Prisma, providing a robust relational database solution.

6.3.2 Using MongoDB with Next.js

Why Use MongoDB?

MongoDB is a **NoSQL document database**, making it ideal for applications that require flexible schemas, high scalability, and fast reads/writes.

Installing Dependencies

bash
```
npm install mongodb
```

Configuring MongoDB Connection

Modify the .env file:

env

```
MONGODB_URI="mongodb+srv://user:password@clus
ter.mongodb.net/mydatabase"
```

Create a new utility file for database connection:

javascript
```
// lib/mongodb.js
import { MongoClient } from "mongodb";

const          client          =          new
MongoClient(process.env.MONGODB_URI);
let db;

export async function connectToDatabase() {
  if (!db) {
    await client.connect();
    db = client.db();
  }
  return db;
}
```

Creating an API Route for Users

Create `pages/api/users.js`:

javascript
```
import  {  connectToDatabase  }  from
"../../lib/mongodb";

export default async function handler(req,
res) {
  const db = await connectToDatabase();
```

```
  const             usersCollection             =
db.collection("users");

  if (req.method === "GET") {
    const          users            =         await
usersCollection.find({}).toArray();
    res.status(200).json(users);
  } else if (req.method === "POST") {
    const { name, email } = req.body;
    if (!name || !email) {
      return  res.status(400).json({  error:
"Name and email are required" });
    }

    const newUser = { name, email };
    await usersCollection.insertOne(newUser);
    res.status(201).json(newUser);
  } else {
    res.status(405).json({ error: "Method Not
Allowed" });
  }
}
```

Testing the API

GET request:

bash
```
curl -X GET http://localhost:3000/api/users
```

POST request:

bash
```bash
curl -X POST http://localhost:3000/api/users -
H   "Content-Type:   application/json"   -d
'{"name": "Bob", "email": "bob@example.com"}'
```

MongoDB is now integrated with Next.js, providing a flexible document-based storage solution.

6.3.3 Using Firebase Firestore with Next.js

Why Use Firebase Firestore?

Firestore is a **serverless NoSQL database** from Firebase, offering **real-time updates, scalability, and easy integration** with frontend applications.

Setting Up Firebase

1. Go to Firebase Console.
2. Create a new project and enable **Firestore Database**.
3. Obtain Firebase credentials from **Project Settings > Service Accounts**.

Installing Dependencies

bash
```bash
npm install firebase-admin
```

Configuring Firebase

Create `lib/firebase.js`:

javascript
```javascript
import admin from "firebase-admin";

const serviceAccount =
JSON.parse(process.env.FIREBASE_SERVICE_ACCOU
NT);

if (!admin.apps.length) {
  admin.initializeApp({
    credential:
admin.credential.cert(serviceAccount),
  });
}

const db = admin.firestore();
export { db };
```

Modify the `.env` file:

env
```env
FIREBASE_SERVICE_ACCOUNT='{
  "type": "service_account",
  "project_id": "your-project-id",
  "private_key": "your-private-key",
  "client_email": "your-client-email"
}'
```

Creating an API Route for Users

Create `pages/api/users.js`:

javascript

```javascript
import { db } from "../../lib/firebase";

export default async function handler(req, res) {
  const usersRef = db.collection("users");

  if (req.method === "GET") {
    const snapshot = await usersRef.get();
    const users = snapshot.docs.map(doc => ({ id: doc.id, ...doc.data() }));
    res.status(200).json(users);
  } else if (req.method === "POST") {
    const { name, email } = req.body;
    if (!name || !email) {
      return res.status(400).json({ error: "Name and email are required" });
    }

    const newUserRef = await usersRef.add({ name, email });
    const newUser = { id: newUserRef.id, name, email };
    res.status(201).json(newUser);
  } else {
    res.status(405).json({ error: "Method Not Allowed" });
  }
}
```

Testing the API

GET request:

bash

```
curl -X GET http://localhost:3000/api/users
```

POST request:

bash

```
curl -X POST http://localhost:3000/api/users -
H   "Content-Type:   application/json"   -d
'{"name":        "Charlie",        "email":
"charlie@example.com"}'
```

Firestore is now integrated with Next.js, providing a serverless and scalable NoSQL database solution.

6.4 Securing API Endpoints with Middleware

Securing API endpoints is essential for protecting sensitive data and ensuring that only authorized users can access specific resources. In this section, you will learn how to implement middleware in Next.js 15 to enforce security policies, including:

- **Authentication**: Restricting access to authenticated users.

- **Authorization**: Controlling access based on user roles and permissions.

- **Rate Limiting**: Preventing abuse by limiting the number of API requests per user.

- **Input Validation**: Ensuring that incoming requests meet expected formats to prevent injection attacks.

By the end of this section, you will be able to secure your Next.js API routes effectively using middleware techniques.

6.4.1 Understanding Middleware in Next.js

Middleware in Next.js allows you to **intercept** requests before they reach the API routes or pages. This is useful for implementing **authentication, logging, request validation, and security policies**.

Creating a Basic Middleware

Next.js 15 provides a built-in middleware system using a `middleware.js` file at the root of the `pages` or `app` directory.

Create `middleware.js` in the root of your project:

javascript

```javascript
import { NextResponse } from "next/server";

export function middleware(req) {
  const token = req.cookies.get("token");

  if (!token) {
```

```
    return              NextResponse.redirect(new
URL("/login", req.url));
  }

  return NextResponse.next();
}

export const config = {
  matcher: "/api/protected/:path*",
};
```

Explanation

- The middleware checks if a **token** is present in the request cookies.

- If no token is found, the user is redirected to the **login page**.

- The `matcher` property ensures that the middleware only applies to routes under `/api/protected/`.

6.4.2 Implementing Authentication Middleware

Using JSON Web Tokens (JWT)

To authenticate users, we will use **JWT (JSON Web Token)** to validate API requests.

Install the Required Dependencies
bash

```
npm install jsonwebtoken
```

Creating an Authentication Middleware

Create `lib/auth.js`:

javascript

```
import jwt from "jsonwebtoken";

export function verifyToken(req) {
  const token = req.cookies.get("token");

  if (!token) return null;

  try {
    return                      jwt.verify(token,
process.env.JWT_SECRET);
  } catch (error) {
    return null;
  }
}
```

Applying Middleware to Secure API Routes

Modify `pages/api/protected/data.js`:

javascript

```
import      {      verifyToken      }      from
"../../../lib/auth";
```

```
export default function handler(req, res) {
  const user = verifyToken(req);

  if (!user) {
    return    res.status(401).json({    error:
"Unauthorized" });
  }

  res.status(200).json({    message:    "Secure
data", user });
}
```

Explanation

- The `verifyToken` function **extracts and verifies the JWT** from cookies.

- If the token is invalid or missing, the API returns a `401 Unauthorized` response.

- If valid, the API returns secure data to the authenticated user.

Testing the API

If no token is provided:

bash
```
curl                    -X                    GET
http://localhost:3000/api/protected/data
```

Response:

json

```
{ "error": "Unauthorized" }
```

If a valid token is provided in cookies, access is granted.

6.4.3 Role-Based Authorization

Why Use Role-Based Access Control (RBAC)?

RBAC ensures that users have access only to the resources they are authorized for. For example:

- **Admin users** can access all API endpoints.
- **Regular users** can access only certain routes.

Updating the Middleware

Modify lib/auth.js to include role verification:

javascript
```
export function verifyToken(req, requiredRole
= null) {
  const token = req.cookies.get("token");
  if (!token) return null;
  try {
    const    user    =    jwt.verify(token,
process.env.JWT_SECRET);

    if   (requiredRole   &&   user.role   !==
requiredRole) {
      return null;
    }
```

```
    return user;
  } catch (error) {
    return null;
  }
}
```

Securing API Routes with Role-Based Access

Modify `pages/api/admin/dashboard.js`:

javascript

```
import { verifyToken } from
"../../../lib/auth";

export default function handler(req, res) {
  const admin = verifyToken(req, "admin");

  if (!admin) {
    return res.status(403).json({ error:
"Forbidden" });
  }

  res.status(200).json({ message: "Admin
dashboard", admin });
}
```

Testing Authorization

Regular users trying to access the admin dashboard will get:

json
```json
{ "error": "Forbidden" }
```

Only users with the **admin** role can access it.

6.4.4 Implementing Rate Limiting

Why Use Rate Limiting?

Rate limiting prevents users from **spamming API endpoints**, reducing the risk of denial-of-service (DoS) attacks.

Installing the `lru-cache` Package

bash
```bash
npm install lru-cache
```

Creating a Rate Limiter

Modify `lib/rateLimit.js`:

javascript
```javascript
import LRU from "lru-cache";
const rateLimitOptions = {
  max: 10, // Allow 10 requests
  ttl: 60000, // Per minute (60,000ms)
};

const rateLimiter = new LRU(rateLimitOptions);

export function rateLimit(req) {
```

```javascript
  const ip = req.headers.get("x-forwarded-
for") || req.ip;

  if (!ip) return false;

  const requestCount = rateLimiter.get(ip) ||
0;

  if (requestCount >= rateLimitOptions.max) {
    return false;
  }

  rateLimiter.set(ip, requestCount + 1,
rateLimitOptions.ttl);
  return true;
}
```

Applying Rate Limiting to API Routes

Modify `pages/api/protected/data.js`:

javascript

```javascript
import { rateLimit } from
"../../../lib/rateLimit";

export default function handler(req, res) {
  if (!rateLimit(req)) {
    return res.status(429).json({ error: "Too
many requests" });
  }
```

```
  res.status(200).json({    message:    "Data
retrieved successfully" });
}
```

Testing Rate Limiting

After **10 requests in a minute**, the API will respond with:

json
```
{ "error": "Too many requests" }
```

6.4.5 Input Validation with Middleware

Why Validate Input?

Validation prevents **SQL injection, XSS attacks, and malformed data** from affecting the database.

Installing the zod Package

bash
```
npm install zod
```

Creating a Validation Middleware

Modify lib/validate.js:

javascript

```
import { z } from "zod";
```

```javascript
const userSchema = z.object({
  name: z.string().min(3),
  email: z.string().email(),
});

export function validateUserInput(req, res,
next) {
  const              result              =
userSchema.safeParse(req.body);

  if (!result.success) {
    return   res.status(400).json({   error:
"Invalid input" });
  }

  next();
}
```

Applying Validation to API Routes

Modify `pages/api/users.js`:

javascript

```javascript
import   {   validateUserInput   }   from
"../../lib/validate";

export default function handler(req, res) {
  if (req.method === "POST") {
    return validateUserInput(req, res, () => {
      res.status(201).json({  message:  "User
created successfully" });
```

```
    });
  }

  res.status(405).json({ error: "Method Not
Allowed" });
}
```

Testing Input Validation

Invalid request:

json
```
{ "error": "Invalid input" }
```

Valid request:

json

```
{ "message": "User created successfully" }
```

Part 3:
Styling, State Management, and Authentication

Chapter 7: Styling in Next.js

Styling is a crucial part of modern web development, influencing both the user experience and application performance. Next.js 15 provides multiple approaches to styling, allowing developers to choose the best method based on project requirements.

In this chapter, you will learn:

- How to use **CSS Modules** for scoped styles.
- How to apply **global styles** effectively.
- How to integrate **Tailwind CSS** for utility-first styling.
- How to leverage **styled-components and Emotion** for dynamic styling.
- Performance considerations and best practices for styling in Next.js.

By the end of this chapter, you will be able to **apply, optimize, and manage styles efficiently in Next.js projects**.

7.1 Using CSS Modules and Global Styles

Styling in Next.js is flexible, supporting various methods, including CSS Modules, global styles, utility-based frameworks like Tailwind CSS, and CSS-in-JS solutions like styled-components and Emotion. This section focuses on **CSS Modules and global styles**, which are two of the most commonly used approaches for styling in Next.js applications.

By the end of this section, you will:

- Understand **CSS Modules** and how they help in **scoped styling**.

- Learn to apply **global styles** effectively while maintaining clean architecture.
- Know how to structure styles in a scalable and maintainable manner.

7.1.1 Understanding CSS Modules

What Are CSS Modules?

CSS Modules allow you to write **component-scoped styles** in Next.js, preventing style conflicts and ensuring better maintainability. Unlike traditional global CSS, CSS Modules generate **unique class names at build time**, making them ideal for styling individual components.

Setting Up CSS Modules

To use CSS Modules in Next.js:

Create a CSS Module file inside the `styles` directory:

bash

```
mkdir styles
touch styles/Button.module.css
```

Define styles in `Button.module.css`:

css

```
/* styles/Button.module.css */
.button {
  background-color: #0070f3;
  color: white;
```

```css
  padding: 10px 20px;
  border-radius: 5px;
  border: none;
  cursor: pointer;
  transition: background-color 0.3s ease-in-out;
}

.button:hover {
  background-color: #005bb5;
}
```

Import and apply styles in a component:
javascript

```javascript
// components/Button.js
import styles from "../styles/Button.module.css";

function Button({ text }) {
  return <button className={styles.button}>{text}</button>;
}

export default Button;
```

Use the component inside a page:

javascript
```javascript
// pages/index.js
import Button from "../components/Button";

export default function Home() {
```

```
  return (
    <div>
      <h1>Welcome to Next.js</h1>
      <Button text="Click Me" />
    </div>
  );
}
```

How CSS Modules Work

At build time, Next.js processes CSS Modules by **generating unique class names** to avoid style conflicts. For example, `.button` might be transformed into:

css
```
.button__1a2b3 {
  background-color: #0070f3;
}
```

This ensures that **styles remain isolated to their respective components**, preventing unintended overrides.

7.1.2 Using Global Styles

Why Use Global Styles?

Global styles are useful for:

- **Defining base styles** (e.g., typography, layouts, resets).

- **Applying consistent theming** across the entire application.

- **Styling elements that span multiple components** (e.g., headers, footers).

However, overusing global styles can lead to **unintended style conflicts**. It is best to combine global styles with CSS Modules to keep styles **organized and maintainable**.

Creating a Global Stylesheet

Create `styles/globals.css`:

css
```css
/* styles/globals.css */
body {
  font-family: Arial, sans-serif;
  margin: 0;
  padding: 0;
  background-color: #f5f5f5;
}

h1 {
  color: #333;
}
```

1.

Import global styles in `_app.js` (for the pages router):

javascript

```javascript
// pages/_app.js
```

```javascript
import "../styles/globals.css";

function MyApp({ Component, pageProps }) {
  return <Component {...pageProps} />;
}

export default MyApp;
```

If using the **App Router (`app` directory)**, import global styles in `layout.js`:

javascript

```javascript
// app/layout.js
import "../styles/globals.css";

export default function RootLayout({ children }) {
  return (
    <html lang="en">
      <body>{children}</body>
    </html>
  );
}
```

2.

Combining Global Styles with CSS Modules

To avoid excessive global styles while maintaining consistency, follow these best practices:

- **Use CSS Modules for component-specific styles.**

- **Keep global styles minimal**, focusing on layout and typography.

- **Organize styles in a structured manner** (e.g., `styles/layout.css`, `styles/theme.css`).

7.1.3 Structuring Styles in a Scalable Manner

For larger applications, structuring styles effectively is essential. Below is a recommended directory structure:

ruby

```
/styles
├── globals.css        # Global styles
├── layout.css         # Layout-specific styles
├── theme.css          # Theme variables and utilities
├── components/
│   ├── Button.module.css  # Scoped styles for components
│   ├── Navbar.module.css  # Scoped styles for Navbar
```

Example: Theming with CSS Variables

To enable **custom themes**, define variables in a separate `theme.css` file:

css

```css
/* styles/theme.css */
:root {
  --primary-color: #0070f3;
  --secondary-color: #ff4081;
  --font-family: Arial, sans-serif;
}

body {
  font-family: var(--font-family);
  background-color: #f5f5f5;
}
```

Import theme.css inside globals.css:

css
```css
@import "./theme.css";
```

Now, styles can be dynamically adjusted using variables:

css
```css
.button {
  background-color: var(--primary-color);
  color: white;
}
```

This approach ensures **maintainability** and allows **easy theme customization**.

7.2 Integrating Tailwind CSS in Next.js

Tailwind CSS is a **utility-first CSS framework** that provides a set of pre-defined classes to rapidly build modern user interfaces without writing custom CSS. It is a popular choice for styling Next.js applications because of its **developer-friendly syntax, responsive utilities, and performance optimizations**.

By the end of this section, you will:

- Understand the **benefits of Tailwind CSS** in Next.js applications.
- Learn how to **install and configure Tailwind CSS** in a Next.js project.
- Apply **responsive design** and **custom styles** using Tailwind utilities.

7.2.1 Why Use Tailwind CSS?

Unlike traditional CSS, where styles are defined in separate stylesheets, Tailwind CSS **applies styles directly via class names** in JSX. This approach offers:

- **Rapid development**: No need to write custom CSS for common styles.
- **Scalability**: Avoids style conflicts by using **utility-based class names**.
- **Built-in responsiveness**: Predefined classes adapt styles across devices.

- **Customization**: Easily configurable via a central `tailwind.config.js` file.

Example comparison:

Traditional CSS:

css
```
/* styles/Button.css */
.button {
  background-color: #0070f3;
  color: white;
  padding: 10px 20px;
  border-radius: 5px;
  border: none;
  cursor: pointer;
}
```

javascript
```
// components/Button.js
import "../styles/Button.css";

function Button({ text }) {
  return                            <button
className="button">{text}</button>;
}
```

Tailwind CSS:

javascript

```
// components/Button.js
function Button({ text }) {
  return (
    <button className="bg-blue-500 text-white
px-4 py-2 rounded-md hover:bg-blue-700">
      {text}
    </button>
  );
}

export default Button;
```

With Tailwind, **styles are defined inline using class names**, eliminating the need for separate stylesheets while ensuring better maintainability.

7.2.2 Installing and Configuring Tailwind CSS

Step 1: Install Tailwind CSS

Inside your Next.js project, run the following command to install Tailwind CSS and its dependencies:

bash
```
npm    install    -D    tailwindcss    postcss
autoprefixer
```

Then, generate the Tailwind configuration files:

bash

```
npx tailwindcss init -p
```

This creates two files:

- `tailwind.config.js` – Tailwind's configuration file.

- `postcss.config.js` – PostCSS configuration for processing Tailwind styles.

Step 2: Configure Tailwind

Open `tailwind.config.js` and update the `content` property to enable Tailwind classes in all components and pages:

javascript

```javascript
// tailwind.config.js
module.exports = {
  content: [
    "./pages/**/*.{js,ts,jsx,tsx}",
    "./components/**/*.{js,ts,jsx,tsx}",
    "./app/**/*.{js,ts,jsx,tsx}",
  ],
  theme: {
    extend: {},
  },
  plugins: [],
};
```

183

This ensures that Tailwind scans the specified directories and removes unused styles in production, improving performance.

Step 3: Add Tailwind to Global Styles

Modify `styles/globals.css` and import Tailwind's base styles:

css

```css
/* styles/globals.css */
@tailwind base;
@tailwind components;
@tailwind utilities;
```

If using the **App Router (app directory)**, import this file inside `layout.js`:

javascript

```javascript
// app/layout.js
import "../styles/globals.css";

export default function RootLayout({ children }) {
  return (
    <html lang="en">
      <body>{children}</body>
    </html>
  );
}
```

For the **Pages Router**, import it in `_app.js`:

javascript

```
// pages/_app.js
import "../styles/globals.css";

function MyApp({ Component, pageProps }) {
  return <Component {...pageProps} />;
}

export default MyApp;
```

At this point, Tailwind CSS is fully integrated and ready to use in your Next.js application.

7.2.3 Using Tailwind CSS in Components

Example 1: Styling a Button

Now that Tailwind is set up, let's create a simple button component using Tailwind classes:

javascript

```
// components/Button.js
function Button({ text }) {
  return (
    <button className="bg-blue-500 text-white
px-4  py-2  rounded-md  hover:bg-blue-700
transition">
```

185

```
      {text}
    </button>
  );
}

export default Button;
```

Here's what each class does:

- `bg-blue-500` – Sets the background color.
- `text-white` – Changes the text color to white.
- `px-4 py-2` – Adds horizontal (`px`) and vertical (`py`) padding.
- `rounded-md` – Applies medium border-radius for rounded corners.
- `hover:bg-blue-700` – Changes background color on hover.
- `transition` – Enables smooth hover transitions.

Use the component in a page:

javascript

```
// pages/index.js
import Button from "../components/Button";

export default function Home() {
  return (
    <div className="flex flex-col items-center justify-center min-h-screen bg-gray-100">
      <h1 className="text-3xl font-bold text-gray-800">Welcome to Next.js</h1>
```

```
      <Button text="Click Me" />
    </div>
  );
}
```

7.2.4 Customizing Tailwind

Tailwind's default styles can be customized using `tailwind.config.js`.

Extending Colors

Modify the `theme.extend` property to add custom colors:

javascript

```
// tailwind.config.js
module.exports = {
  theme: {
    extend: {
      colors: {
        primary: "#4CAF50", // Custom green
        secondary: "#FF5722", // Custom orange
      },
    },
  },
};
```

Now, you can use these colors in your components:

javascript

```
<button className="bg-primary text-white px-4
py-2 rounded-md hover:bg-secondary">
  Custom Button
</button>
```

7.2.5 Responsive Design with Tailwind

Tailwind makes **responsive design simple** with its mobile-first approach.

Example: Responsive Grid Layout

javascript

```
// pages/index.js
export default function Home() {
  return (
    <div className="grid grid-cols-1 md:grid-
cols-2 lg:grid-cols-3 gap-4 p-4">
      <div className="bg-white p-6 shadow-md
rounded-md">Item 1</div>
      <div className="bg-white p-6 shadow-md
rounded-md">Item 2</div>
      <div className="bg-white p-6 shadow-md
rounded-md">Item 3</div>
    </div>
  );
}
```

Breakdown:

- `grid-cols-1` – **Single column on small screens**.

- `md:grid-cols-2` – **Two columns on medium screens** (`md` **breakpoint**).

- `lg:grid-cols-3` – **Three columns on large screens (`lg` breakpoint)**.

- `gap-4` – Adds spacing between grid items.

Tailwind's responsive utilities allow quick adjustments without writing custom media queries.

7.3 Styled-Components and Emotion for Dynamic Styling

In addition to utility-first CSS frameworks like Tailwind, Next.js supports component-based styling using **CSS-in-JS** libraries such as **styled-components** and **Emotion**. These libraries allow developers to write **encapsulated, dynamic, and themeable styles** directly within JavaScript components.

By the end of this section, you will:

- Understand the **differences between styled-components and Emotion**.
- Learn how to **install and configure both libraries** in a Next.js project.
- Apply **dynamic styling** using props, themes, and global styles.

7.3.1 Why Use CSS-in-JS?

Traditional CSS and utility-first frameworks work well, but CSS-in-JS libraries offer unique advantages:

- **Scoped styles**: Styles are component-specific, avoiding global conflicts.

- **Dynamic styling**: Supports conditional logic, props, and theme-based styling.

- **Server-side rendering (SSR) support**: Both styled-components and Emotion integrate seamlessly with Next.js SSR.

- **Component encapsulation**: Styles remain tied to the component logic, improving maintainability.

These benefits make CSS-in-JS a powerful approach for styling modern Next.js applications.

7.3.2 Installing and Setting Up Styled-Components

Step 1: Install Dependencies

Run the following command to install styled-components and its required dependencies:

bash
```
npm install styled-components
```

```
npm install -D babel-plugin-styled-components
```

The `babel-plugin-styled-components` package **improves debugging and server-side rendering support** in Next.js.

Step 2: Configure Babel

Create or update the `.babelrc` file in the root directory:

json
```
{
  "presets": ["next/babel"],
  "plugins":          ["babel-plugin-styled-
components"]
}
```

This configuration ensures styled-components work correctly in both development and production modes.

Step 3: Create a Styled Component

Now, create a simple styled button component using styled-components.

javascript
```
// components/Button.js
import styled from "styled-components";

const Button = styled.button`
```

```
  background-color:         ${(props)         =>
(props.primary ? "#0070f3" : "#ddd")};
  color: ${(props) => (props.primary ? "white"
: "black")};
  padding: 10px 20px;
  border-radius: 5px;
  border: none;
  cursor: pointer;
  transition: background-color 0.3s;

  &:hover {
    background-color:         ${(props)         =>
(props.primary ? "#0056b3" : "#bbb")};
  }
`;

export default Button;
```

Key Features:

- Uses **template literals** for defining styles.

- Accepts **props (`primary`)** to toggle styles dynamically.

- Implements **hover effects** using the `&:hover` selector.

Step 4: Use the Styled Component in a Page

Modify `pages/index.js` to include the styled button:

javascript

```javascript
// pages/index.js
import Button from "../components/Button";

export default function Home() {
  return (
    <div style={{ textAlign: "center",
marginTop: "50px" }}>
      <h1>Styled-Components in Next.js</h1>
      <Button primary>Primary Button</Button>
      <Button>Secondary Button</Button>
    </div>
  );
}
```

Styled-components generate **unique class names** for each instance, ensuring styles remain **scoped and conflict-free**.

Step 5: Adding Global Styles

Global styles can be applied using the `createGlobalStyle` function.

javascript

```javascript
// components/GlobalStyles.js
import { createGlobalStyle } from "styled-components";

const GlobalStyles = createGlobalStyle`
```

193

```
  body {
    font-family: Arial, sans-serif;
    margin: 0;
    padding: 0;
    background-color: #f5f5f5;
  }
`;

export default GlobalStyles;
```

Now, import this into pages/_app.js (if using the Pages Router) or app/layout.js (if using the App Router).

javascript

```
// pages/_app.js
import         GlobalStyles         from
"../components/GlobalStyles";

function MyApp({ Component, pageProps }) {
  return (
    <>
      <GlobalStyles />
      <Component {...pageProps} />
    </>
  );
}

export default MyApp;
```

7.3.3 Installing and Setting Up Emotion

Emotion is another powerful CSS-in-JS library that offers **better performance and advanced styling capabilities**.

Step 1: Install Dependencies

Run the following command to install Emotion:

bash

```
npm install @emotion/react @emotion/styled
```

Step 2: Create a Styled Component

With Emotion, components are styled similarly to styled-components.

javascript

```
// components/Card.js
import styled from "@emotion/styled";

const Card = styled.div`
  background: white;
  padding: 20px;
  border-radius: 8px;
  box-shadow: 0px 4px 6px rgba(0, 0, 0, 0.1);
  max-width: 300px;
  text-align: center;
`;

const Title = styled.h2`
```

195

```
  color:    ${(props)   =>   (props.color   ?
props.color : "#333")};
`;

export default function CardComponent() {
  return (
    <Card>
      <Title    color="#0070f3">Emotion    in
Next.js</Title>
      <p>Styled with Emotion.</p>
    </Card>
  );
}
```

Key Features:

- Uses **template literals** to define styles.
- Supports **dynamic props** (`color`).
- Works similarly to styled-components but with **lighter runtime overhead**.

Step 3: Use the Styled Component in a Page

Import the `CardComponent` in a Next.js page:

javascript

```
// pages/index.js
import         CardComponent         from
"../components/Card";
```

196

```javascript
export default function Home() {
  return (
    <div    style={{    display:    "flex",
justifyContent:  "center",  marginTop:  "50px"
}}>
      <CardComponent />
    </div>
  );
}
```

7.3.4 Theming with Emotion

Emotion provides a built-in theming system via the ThemeProvider.

Step 1: Define a Theme

Create a theme.js file:

javascript
```
// styles/theme.js
const theme = {
  colors: {
    primary: "#0070f3",
    secondary: "#ff4081",
  },
};
export default theme;
```

Step 2: Apply the Theme

Use ThemeProvider to wrap the application:

javascript

```javascript
// pages/_app.js
import { ThemeProvider } from
"@emotion/react";
import theme from "../styles/theme";

function MyApp({ Component, pageProps }) {
  return (
    <ThemeProvider theme={theme}>
      <Component {...pageProps} />
    </ThemeProvider>
  );
}

export default MyApp;
```

Step 3: Use Theme Values in Components

Modify Card.js to use theme colors:

javascript

```javascript
import styled from "@emotion/styled";

const Title = styled.h2`
  color: ${(props) =>
props.theme.colors.primary};
`;

export default function CardComponent() {
```

198

```
return (
  <div>
    <Title>Emotion with Theme</Title>
    <p>Using a global theme.</p>
  </div>
);
}
```

7.4 Performance Considerations in Styling

Styling plays a crucial role in the performance of Next.js applications. While modern styling techniques like CSS Modules, Styled-Components, and Emotion provide flexibility and maintainability, improper usage can negatively impact **rendering speed, load times, and overall application performance**.

This section explores key **performance considerations** when working with styles in Next.js. By the end of this section, you will:

- Understand how different styling approaches affect **client-side and server-side performance**.
- Learn best practices to **reduce unnecessary re-renders, optimize CSS delivery, and minimize bundle size**.
- Implement **performance-oriented styling techniques** to enhance the user experience.

7.4.1 Evaluating Styling Approaches for Performance

Each styling approach in Next.js comes with **trade-offs in performance**. Below is a comparison of commonly used styling methods:

Styling Method	Pros	Cons
CSS Modules	Small bundle size, static extraction, fast rendering	Requires additional setup for global styles
Styled-Components	Component-scoped styles, dynamic theming	Higher runtime cost, additional client-side processing
Emotion	Lightweight, supports SSR, flexible	Slightly more runtime overhead than CSS Modules
Tailwind CSS	Highly optimized, utility-first, minimal runtime cost	Large stylesheet if not purged correctly

For **best performance**, it is recommended to **use static styles (CSS Modules, Tailwind)** when possible and **limit runtime styling (Styled-Components, Emotion) to dynamic scenarios**.

7.4.2 Server-Side Rendering (SSR) and Styling

Next.js applications benefit from **server-side rendering (SSR)**, but improper styling techniques can lead to **Flash of Unstyled Content (FOUC)** and performance bottlenecks.

Avoiding Flash of Unstyled Content (FOUC)

When using **CSS-in-JS libraries** like styled-components or Emotion, styles are often generated **at runtime**, causing a delay in applying styles during SSR.

To prevent this:

- Ensure **critical CSS is preloaded** to avoid layout shifts.
- Use **static extraction** for styles where possible.
- Configure **SSR support for CSS-in-JS libraries** to render styles on the server.

For styled-components, update _document.js to include SSR support:

javascript
```
// pages/_document.js
import Document from "next/document";
import { ServerStyleSheet } from "styled-components";

export default class MyDocument extends Document {
  static async getInitialProps(ctx) {
    const sheet = new ServerStyleSheet();
    const originalRenderPage = ctx.renderPage;

    try {
```

```
    ctx.renderPage = () =>
      originalRenderPage({
        enhanceApp: (App) => (props) =>
sheet.collectStyles(<App {...props} />),
      });

    const   initialProps   =   await
Document.getInitialProps(ctx);
      return {
        ...initialProps,
        styles: (
          <>
            {initialProps.styles}
            {sheet.getStyleElement()}
          </>
        ),
      };
    } finally {
      sheet.seal();
    }
  }
}
```

This ensures that styled-components **render styles server-side**, preventing FOUC.

Similarly, for Emotion, install and configure @emotion/server for SSR support.

7.4.3 Reducing Unnecessary Re-Renders

Dynamic styling can cause **unnecessary re-renders** if not optimized correctly.

Common Performance Issues

Passing   inline   styles   inside   components

javascript

```
function Button() {
  return <button style={{ backgroundColor:
"blue" }}>Click Me</button>;
}
```

1.

  ○ Inline styles create **new objects on each render**, causing re-renders.

Using functions in styled-components without memoization

javascript

```
const Button = styled.button`
  background-color: ${(props) => props.primary
? "blue" : "gray"};
`;
```

2.

  ○ If used inside a parent component that re-renders frequently, it **creates new style objects unnecessarily**.

Optimizing for Performance

- **Use memoization** with useMemo for computed styles.

- **Avoid unnecessary dynamic styles** when static styles can be used.

- **Use pure components** to prevent unnecessary updates.

Example: Optimized styled-component with useMemo:

javascript

```javascript
import { useMemo } from "react";
import styled from "styled-components";

const StyledButton = styled.button`
  background-color:         ${(props)         =>
props.bgColor};
  color: white;
  padding: 10px 20px;
  border: none;
`;

export default function Button({ primary }) {
  const bgColor = useMemo(() => (primary ?
"blue" : "gray"), [primary]);

  return                                <StyledButton
bgColor={bgColor}>Click Me</StyledButton>;
}
```

By using useMemo, **the computed value persists across renders**, improving performance.

7.4.4 Optimizing CSS Delivery

Reducing Unused CSS

Large CSS files **increase page load times**. Techniques to reduce unused CSS:

- **Enable PurgeCSS with Tailwind CSS** to remove unused styles.

- **Use code-splitting** to load styles only when needed.

- **Minimize global styles**, keeping most styles scoped to components.

Enabling PurgeCSS in Tailwind

Modify `tailwind.config.js`:

javascript

```javascript
module.exports = {
  purge:                      ["./pages/**/*.js",
"./components/**/*.js"],
  theme: {
    extend: {},
  },
  plugins: [],
};
```

This removes unused CSS **before production build**, reducing file size.

Using Critical CSS for Faster Rendering

Critical CSS **inlines only the necessary styles** for above-the-fold content, improving performance.

Enable automatic critical CSS optimization in Next.js by setting:

javascript

```
module.exports = {
  experimental: {
    optimizeCss: true,
  },
};
```

Next.js automatically extracts and inlines critical styles, **reducing initial load time**.

Lazy Loading Non-Critical Styles

For large stylesheets, **lazy-load styles** only when needed.

javascript

```
import dynamic from "next/dynamic";

const    Styles    =    dynamic(()    =>
import("../styles/extraStyles.module.css"), {
```

```
  ssr: false,
});

export default function Page() {
  return (
    <div>
      <h1  className={Styles.title}>Optimized
Styling</h1>
    </div>
  );
}
```

By disabling SSR (`ssr: false`), styles are **loaded only when the component mounts**, reducing **initial load size**.

7.4.5 Minimizing Bundle Size

Avoid Large CSS-in-JS Libraries

CSS-in-JS libraries like styled-components **increase bundle size**. If dynamic styles are not required, prefer:

- **CSS Modules**

- **Tailwind CSS**

- **Static stylesheets (global.css)**

To analyze bundle size, use:

bash

```
npm run analyze
```

This enables Next.js' **webpack bundle analyzer** to identify large dependencies.

Removing Unused Libraries

Run the following command to detect unused dependencies:

bash

```
npx depcheck
```

If unnecessary libraries like `styled-components` or `emotion` are installed but unused, **remove them** to reduce bundle size.

Chapter 8: State Management in Next.js

State management is a crucial aspect of building dynamic and interactive web applications. In Next.js, managing state effectively ensures smooth user interactions, efficient updates, and optimal performance.

In this chapter, we will explore **different state management techniques** in Next.js, including:

- **React Context API** for local state management
- **Redux Toolkit** for global state management
- **Zustand and Recoil** as lightweight alternatives to Redux
- **Best practices for optimizing state performance**

By the end of this chapter, you will have a **deep understanding of state management in Next.js applications** and be able to choose the right approach based on your project's complexity and scalability needs.

8.1 Using React Context API for Local State

State management is an essential part of any web application, as it determines how data flows and updates across components. In Next.js applications, local state management is often needed to maintain user preferences, authentication status, UI themes, and other shared data.

The **React Context API** is a built-in solution that enables state sharing between components **without prop drilling**. It is particularly useful for managing **application-wide state** that is not complex enough to require a full-fledged state management library like Redux.

In this section, we will cover:

- What the **React Context API** is and when to use it
- How to **create and use a Context Provider** in Next.js
- Implementing a **real-world example** of theme switching
- **Limitations and best practices** for using the Context API

By the end of this section, you will have a solid understanding of how to use the Context API in a Next.js application.

8.1.1 Understanding the React Context API

What is the Context API?

The **Context API** is a built-in feature in React that allows **data to be passed through the component tree without manually passing props at every level**.

When Should You Use the Context API?

The Context API is useful for:

- **Global state management for small to medium-sized applications**

- **Theme switching (light/dark mode)**

- **Authentication state (user login sessions)**

- **Managing language and localization settings**

However, for **large-scale applications with frequent state updates**, Redux Toolkit or Zustand may be a better choice due to better performance optimizations.

8.1.2 Implementing Context API in Next.js

Let's build a **theme toggle system** using the Context API in a Next.js 15 application. This example will allow users to switch between **light** and **dark** themes.

Step 1: Creating a Context Provider

First, create a **context file** to manage theme state.

File: `context/ThemeContext.js`

javascript

```javascript
import { createContext, useState, useContext }
from "react";

// Create the ThemeContext

const ThemeContext = createContext();

// Create a provider component

export function ThemeProvider({ children }) {

  const [theme, setTheme] = useState("light");

  // Toggle theme function

  const toggleTheme = () => {

    setTheme((prevTheme)  =>  (prevTheme  ===
"light" ? "dark" : "light"));

  };
```

```
  return (

    <ThemeContext.Provider    value={{    theme,
toggleTheme }}>

      {children}

    </ThemeContext.Provider>

  );

}

// Custom hook for easier context consumption

export function useTheme() {

  return useContext(ThemeContext);

}
```

Explanation:

- ThemeContext is created using createContext().
- ThemeProvider manages the state (theme) and provides a function (toggleTheme) to update it.
- useTheme() is a custom hook that makes it easier to access theme data in components.

Step 2: Wrapping the Application with the Provider

To ensure the theme state is available across the application, wrap the `_app.js` file with `ThemeProvider`.

File: `pages/_app.js`

javascript

```javascript
import { ThemeProvider } from "../context/ThemeContext";

function MyApp({ Component, pageProps }) {

  return (

    <ThemeProvider>

      <Component {...pageProps} />

    </ThemeProvider>

  );

}

export default MyApp;
```

Why is this necessary?

Wrapping the entire application inside `ThemeProvider` ensures that the **theme state is accessible from any component**.

Step 3: Using Context in Components

Now, let's create a button that toggles between light and dark mode.

File: `components/ThemeToggle.js`

javascript

```javascript
import { useTheme } from "../context/ThemeContext";

export default function ThemeToggle() {
  const { theme, toggleTheme } = useTheme();

  return (

    <button onClick={toggleTheme}>

      Switch to {theme === "light" ? "dark" : "light"} mode

    </button>

  );

}
```

How it works:

- `useTheme()` is used to access the `theme` state and `toggleTheme` function.
- When the button is clicked, `toggleTheme()` updates the theme.

Step 4: Applying Theme Styles

Let's use the theme state to change the **background color** dynamically.

Modify the **global CSS file** to define light and dark themes.

File: styles/globals.css

css

```css
body {

  transition:  background-color  0.3s  ease,
color 0.3s ease;

}

.light {

  background-color: #ffffff;

  color: #000000;

}

.dark {

  background-color: #121212;

  color: #ffffff;

}
```

Then, apply the theme dynamically in the pages/index.js file.

File: pages/index.js

215

javascript

```javascript
import { useTheme } from
"../context/ThemeContext";

import ThemeToggle from
"../components/ThemeToggle";

export default function Home() {

  const { theme } = useTheme();

  return (

    <div className={theme}>

      <h1>Welcome to Next.js</h1>

      <ThemeToggle />

    </div>

  );

}
```

Now, when you toggle the theme, the background color updates instantly.

8.1.3 Best Practices and Limitations

Best Practices

- **Use Context API only for truly shared state.**

- If only a few components need the state, passing props may be simpler.

- **Use a custom hook (`useTheme( )`) for better code organization.**

- **Combine Context API with local state when needed.**

  - The Context API is not meant to replace `useState`, but rather to **share** state.

Limitations

- **Performance concerns**:
  - Every state update causes **all consuming components to re-render**.
  - For frequently updated states (e.g., live chat messages), Redux or Zustand may perform better.

- **Complexity in large applications**:
  - Using multiple contexts can become difficult to manage.

8.1.4 When to Use Context API vs. Other State Management Solutions

Feature	Context API	Redux Toolkit	Zustand

Complexity	Low (simple setup)	High (boilerplate)	Medium (minimal setup)
Performance	Medium (re-renders)	High (efficient updates)	High (optimized updates)
Use Case	Local state, themes, auth	Large-scale global state	Small to medium-sized apps
Ease of Use	Easy	Complex	Easy

For small to medium applications, **Context API** is often sufficient. However, for **scalable global state management**, Redux Toolkit or Zustand should be considered.

8.2 Integrating Redux Toolkit for Global State Management

As web applications grow in complexity, managing **global state** efficiently becomes a critical challenge. While React's Context API works well for **local state management**, it has limitations when dealing with **frequent state updates** or **large-scale applications**.

Redux Toolkit (RTK) is the **official, recommended way** to manage state in Redux applications. It provides a **simplified API**, **improves performance**, and reduces **boilerplate code**, making it an ideal choice for **Next.js applications** that require a **scalable state management solution**.

In this section, we will cover:

- What **Redux Toolkit** is and why it is preferred over traditional Redux
- How to **integrate Redux Toolkit** into a Next.js 15 application
- Implementing a **global state for user authentication** using RTK
- **Best practices** for using Redux Toolkit in Next.js

By the end of this section, you will have a solid understanding of **Redux Toolkit's role in Next.js applications** and how to use it effectively.

8.2.1 Understanding Redux Toolkit

What is Redux Toolkit?

Redux Toolkit (RTK) is a **state management library** that simplifies the use of Redux. It provides:

- **A streamlined API** that reduces boilerplate
- **Built-in support for immutable updates** using Immer.js
- **Efficient state updates** with automatic performance optimizations

- **Asynchronous state management** via `createAsyncThunk`

Why Use Redux Toolkit Instead of Context API?

While **React Context API** is great for small-scale state management, it has **performance drawbacks** when dealing with:

Feature	Context API	Redux Toolkit
State Scope	Local/global	Global
Performance	Re-renders all consumers	Optimized updates
Ease of Use	Simple	Slightly more setup
Middleware Support	Limited	Extensive

For applications with **complex state logic**, **frequent updates**, or **server-side data fetching**, Redux Toolkit is the **better choice**.

8.2.2 Setting Up Redux Toolkit in Next.js

Step 1: Installing Redux Toolkit

To start using Redux Toolkit in a Next.js 15 project, install the required dependencies:

sh

```
npm install @reduxjs/toolkit react-redux
```

- `@reduxjs/toolkit` provides the Redux functionality.

- `react-redux` allows React components to interact with the Redux store.

Step 2: Creating a Redux Store

In Next.js, the store should be initialized in a separate file.

File: `store/index.js`

javascript

```
import { configureStore } from
"@reduxjs/toolkit";

import authReducer from "./slices/authSlice";

export const store = configureStore({

  reducer: {
```

```
    auth: authReducer,

  },

});
```

Explanation:

- `configureStore()` sets up the Redux store with built-in **middleware** and **DevTools integration**.

- `authReducer` will handle user authentication state.

Step 3: Creating an Authentication Slice

Redux Toolkit introduces **slices**, which contain the **state, reducers, and actions** in a single file.

File: `store/slices/authSlice.js`

javascript

```javascript
import { createSlice } from
"@reduxjs/toolkit";

const initialState = {

  user: null,

  isAuthenticated: false,

};
```

```
const authSlice = createSlice({

  name: "auth",

  initialState,

  reducers: {

    login: (state, action) => {

      state.user = action.payload;

      state.isAuthenticated = true;

    },

    logout: (state) => {

      state.user = null;

      state.isAuthenticated = false;

    },

  },

});

export const { login, logout } =
authSlice.actions;

export default authSlice.reducer;
```

How it works:

- createSlice() generates **action creators and reducers** automatically.

- The login() action updates the user state.

- The logout() action clears the authentication state.

Step 4: Providing the Store in Next.js

To make the Redux store accessible throughout the app, wrap the application with the Provider component in _app.js.

File: pages/_app.js

javascript

```javascript
import { Provider } from "react-redux";
import { store } from "../store";
function MyApp({ Component, pageProps }) {
  return (
    <Provider store={store}>
      <Component {...pageProps} />
    </Provider>
  );
}
```

```
export default MyApp;
```

Why is this necessary?

- The `Provider` component ensures that **Redux state is available globally** in the application.

8.2.3 Using Redux State in Components

Now, let's create a **login/logout button** that interacts with Redux state.

Step 1: Accessing Redux State

Use Redux **selectors and dispatch functions** inside components.

File: `components/AuthStatus.js`

javascript

```
import { useSelector, useDispatch } from
"react-redux";

import { login, logout } from
"../store/slices/authSlice";

export default function AuthStatus() {

  const dispatch = useDispatch();

  const { user, isAuthenticated } =
useSelector((state) => state.auth);
```

```
  return (

    <div>

      {isAuthenticated ? (

        <>

          <p>Welcome, {user.name}!</p>

          <button        onClick={()        =>
dispatch(logout())}>Logout</button>

        </>

      ) : (

        <button        onClick={()        =>
dispatch(login({ name: "John Doe" }))}>

          Login

        </button>

      )}

    </div>

  );

}
```

Explanation:

- useSelector() retrieves the authentication state.
- useDispatch() triggers **login** and **logout** actions.

- Clicking the **login button** updates the Redux state with a mock user.
- Clicking **logout** clears the user state.

Step 2: Displaying Authentication Status

Modify `pages/index.js` to display authentication status.

File: `pages/index.js`

javascript

```
import AuthStatus from
"../components/AuthStatus";

export default function Home() {

  return (

    <div>

      <h1>Next.js with Redux Toolkit</h1>

      <AuthStatus />

    </div>

  );

}
```

Now, when you click **login**, the state updates, and the UI reflects the change.

8.2.4 Best Practices for Using Redux Toolkit in Next.js

1. Keep Slices Small and Modular

- Organize state into **separate slices** (`authSlice.js`, `cartSlice.js`, etc.).

2. Use `createAsyncThunk` for API Calls

- Handle asynchronous requests inside Redux slices.

Example:

javascript

```javascript
import { createAsyncThunk, createSlice } from
"@reduxjs/toolkit";

export const fetchUser =
createAsyncThunk("auth/fetchUser", async () =>
{

  const response = await fetch("/api/user");

  return await response.json();

});
```

```javascript
const authSlice = createSlice({

  name: "auth",

  initialState: { user: null, status: "idle"
},

  reducers: {},

  extraReducers: (builder) => {

    builder

      .addCase(fetchUser.pending, (state) => {

        state.status = "loading";

      })

      .addCase(fetchUser.fulfilled,    (state,
action) => {

        state.status = "succeeded";

        state.user = action.payload;

      });

  },

});

export default authSlice.reducer;
```

3. Optimize Performance with Memoization

- Use `useMemo()` and `useCallback()` to **prevent unnecessary re-renders**.

4. Use Middleware for Advanced Features

- Add `redux-thunk` or `redux-saga` for side effects.

8.3 Using Zustand and Recoil for Simpler State Management

While **Redux Toolkit** is a powerful solution for global state management in **Next.js**, it may introduce unnecessary complexity for small to medium-sized applications. In many cases, developers prefer **simpler state management solutions** that require less boilerplate and are easier to integrate.

Two popular alternatives to Redux Toolkit are:

- **Zustand** – A lightweight state management library with a simple API.
- **Recoil** – A state management library developed by Facebook that integrates seamlessly with React components.

In this section, we will explore both libraries, how they work, and how to integrate them into a Next.js 15 application.

8.3.1 Understanding Zustand

What is Zustand?

Zustand is a **minimalist and fast** state management library that offers:

- **A simple API** with minimal boilerplate

- **Global state persistence** without reducers

- **Direct mutation** without complex actions

- **Optimized performance** with selective re-renders

Unlike Redux, Zustand does not require context providers or reducers, making it a great choice for **smaller Next.js applications** or **components that require lightweight state management**.

8.3.2 Integrating Zustand into Next.js

Step 1: Installing Zustand

Install Zustand using npm or yarn:

sh

```
npm install zustand
```

Step 2: Creating a Zustand Store

Zustand stores are **functions** that return state and state-modifying functions.

File: `store/useAuthStore.js`

javascript

```
import { create } from "zustand";

const useAuthStore = create((set) => ({

  user: null,

  isAuthenticated: false,

  login:    (user)    =>    set({    user,
isAuthenticated: true }),

  logout:    ()    =>    set({    user:    null,
isAuthenticated: false }),

}));

export default useAuthStore;
```

How it works:

- `create()` initializes a Zustand store.
- The store maintains `user` and `isAuthenticated` state.
- `login()` updates the state with user details.
- `logout()` resets the state.

Step 3: Using Zustand in a Component

To access and modify the state, use the **Zustand hook** inside components.

File: components/AuthStatus.js

javascript

```
import            useAuthStore            from
"../store/useAuthStore";

export default function AuthStatus() {

  const { user, isAuthenticated, login, logout
} = useAuthStore();

  return (

    <div>

      {isAuthenticated ? (

        <>

          <p>Welcome, {user.name}!</p>

          <button
onClick={logout}>Logout</button>

        </>

      ) : (
```

233

```
        <button onClick={() => login({ name:
"John Doe" })}>Login</button>

      )}

    </div>

  );

}
```

Why use Zustand?

- **No need for a Provider** – Zustand does not require wrapping the app in a context provider.

- **Minimal boilerplate** – No reducers, actions, or dispatch functions are needed.

Step 4: Displaying Authentication Status

Modify pages/index.js to display the authentication state.

File: pages/index.js

javascript

```
import                AuthStatus                from
"../components/AuthStatus";

export default function Home() {

  return (
```

```
<div>

  <h1>Next.js with Zustand</h1>

  <AuthStatus />

</div>

  );

}
```

At this point, clicking the **login** button updates the Zustand state, and clicking **logout** resets it.

8.3.3 Understanding Recoil

What is Recoil?

Recoil is a state management library developed by **Facebook (Meta)** that:

- **Provides fine-grained reactivity** (components only update when needed).

- **Integrates seamlessly with React** and the Context API.

- **Works well with Next.js Server Components**.

Unlike Zustand, Recoil **requires a provider** but offers **atomic state management**, making it useful for **component-scoped and global state**.

8.3.4 Integrating Recoil into Next.js

Step 1: Installing Recoil

Install Recoil with:

sh

```
npm install recoil
```

Step 2: Creating a Recoil Store

Recoil state is managed using **atoms** (shared state) and **selectors** (computed state).

File: `store/authAtom.js`

javascript

```
import { atom } from "recoil";

export const authState = atom({
  key: "authState",
  default: {
    user: null,
    isAuthenticated: false,
  },
```

```
});
```

How it works:

- `atom()` creates a piece of global state.

- The `authState` atom stores the authentication status.

Step 3: Providing the Recoil Root

To use Recoil, wrap the application with the `RecoilRoot` component.

File: `pages/_app.js`

javascript

```javascript
import { RecoilRoot } from "recoil";

function MyApp({ Component, pageProps }) {

  return (

    <RecoilRoot>

      <Component {...pageProps} />

    </RecoilRoot>

  );

}
```

```
export default MyApp;
```

Step 4: Using Recoil State in a Component

Use the useRecoilState hook to **access and update state.**

File: components/AuthStatus.js

javascript

```
import { useRecoilState } from "recoil";

import { authState } from "../store/authAtom";

export default function AuthStatus() {

  const        [auth,        setAuth]        =
useRecoilState(authState);


  return (

    <div>

      {auth.isAuthenticated ? (

        <>

          <p>Welcome, {auth.user.name}!</p>

          <button  onClick={()  =>  setAuth({
user: null, isAuthenticated: false })}>
```

```
        Logout

      </button>

    </>

  ) : (

      <button onClick={() => setAuth({ user:
{ name: "John Doe" }, isAuthenticated: true
})}>

        Login

      </button>

    )}

  </div>

 );

}
```

Why use Recoil?

- **Fine-grained updates** – Components re-render **only when necessary**.
- **Scoped state management** – Great for local and global state.

Step 5: Displaying Authentication Status

Modify pages/index.js to display authentication status.

File: `pages/index.js`

javascript

```
import              AuthStatus              from
"../components/AuthStatus";

export default function Home() {

  return (

    <div>

      <h1>Next.js with Recoil</h1>

      <AuthStatus />

    </div>

  );

}
```

Now, clicking the **login** button updates the Recoil atom, and clicking
logout resets it.

8.3.5 Choosing Between Zustand and Recoil

Feature	Zustand	Recoil
Boilerplate	Minimal	Moderate

Provider Required	No	Yes
Performance	High	Optimized
Ease of Use	Simple	Moderate
Best Use Case	Small apps, UI state	Global state, computed values

When to Choose Zustand

- If you **prefer minimal boilerplate** and **direct state mutations**.
- If you need **lightweight global state management**.

When to Choose Recoil

- If your app requires **fine-grained reactivity**.
- If you want **atomic state management** with dependency tracking.

8.4 Best Practices for Optimizing State Performance

Efficient state management is crucial for maintaining **high performance and scalability** in Next.js applications. Poorly optimized state can lead to **unnecessary re-renders, slow performance, and**

memory leaks. This section covers best practices to ensure state management remains **efficient, responsive, and scalable**.

We will explore:

- **Minimizing unnecessary re-renders**

- **Using context providers efficiently**

- **Optimizing global and local state**

- **Leveraging memoization techniques**

- **Choosing the right state management approach**

8.4.1 Minimizing Unnecessary Re-Renders

Understanding React's Rendering Behavior

In React, components re-render when:

1. **State changes** – If a component's state updates, it re-renders.

2. **Props change** – If a parent component passes new props, the child re-renders.

3. **Context updates** – If a context provider updates, all consumers re-render.

Unoptimized state can cause **deep re-render chains**, leading to performance degradation.

Best Practices to Reduce Re-Renders

1. Split Large State into Smaller Pieces

Instead of storing an entire application's state in a **single provider**, break it down into **multiple specialized providers**.

Inefficient Approach:

javascript

```javascript
const AppContext = createContext({ user: null,
theme: "light", cart: [] });

function AppProvider({ children }) {

  const [state, setState] = useState({ user:
null, theme: "light", cart: [] });

  return (

    <AppContext.Provider    value={{    state,
setState }}>

      {children}

    </AppContext.Provider>

  );

}
```

This approach causes **all components** consuming AppContext to **re-render whenever any state property changes**.

Optimized Approach:

javascript

```javascript
const UserContext = createContext(null);

const ThemeContext = createContext("light");

function UserProvider({ children }) {

  const [user, setUser] = useState(null);

  return (

    <UserContext.Provider    value={{    user,
setUser }}>

      {children}

    </UserContext.Provider>

  );

}


function ThemeProvider({ children }) {

  const [theme, setTheme] = useState("light");

  return (
```

```
    <ThemeContext.Provider   value={{   theme,
setTheme }}>

      {children}

    </ThemeContext.Provider>

  );

}
```

By splitting state, **only relevant parts of the application re-render** when necessary.

---

2. **Use** useMemo **and** useCallback **for Expensive Computations**

- useMemo prevents expensive recalculations unless dependencies change.
- useCallback memoizes functions to prevent unnecessary re-creations.

Example: Optimizing Computed Values with useMemo

javascript

```
const expensiveCalculation = useMemo(() => {

  return items.reduce((total, item) => total +
item.price, 0);

}, [items]);
```

Example: Optimizing Callback Functions with useCallback

javascript

```javascript
const handleClick = useCallback(() => {
  console.log("Button clicked!");
}, []);
```

8.4.2 Using Context Providers Efficiently

1. Avoid Overusing Context

React Context is powerful but **should not be used for frequently changing state** (e.g., form inputs, animations). Instead, **local state or a lightweight state library** like Zustand is preferable.

2. Use Selective Context Consumption

Instead of consuming **entire context objects**, extract only the necessary values.

Inefficient Approach:

javascript

```javascript
const { user, theme } = useContext(AppContext);
```

This causes **unnecessary re-renders** when **either** user or theme changes.

Optimized Approach:

javascript

```javascript
const user = useContext(UserContext);

const theme = useContext(ThemeContext);
```

Now, changes in `UserContext` **do not affect** components using `ThemeContext`.

8.4.3 Optimizing Global and Local State

1. Store Global State Only When Necessary

- **Global state** should be used for data **shared across multiple components** (e.g., authentication, theme).

- **Local state** should be used for **component-specific** data (e.g., form inputs, modal visibility).

Example: Storing User Authentication Globally

javascript

```javascript
const AuthContext = createContext(null);

function AuthProvider({ children }) {

  const [user, setUser] = useState(null);

  return (

    <AuthContext.Provider    value={{    user,
setUser }}>
```

```
      {children}

    </AuthContext.Provider>

  );

}
```

---

2. Use Lazy Initialization for State

Lazy initialization prevents unnecessary computations **on initial render**.

Inefficient:

javascript

```javascript
const [data, setData] = useState(fetchData());
// Runs fetchData() on every render
```

Optimized:

javascript

```javascript
const [data, setData] = useState(() =>
fetchData()); // Runs fetchData() only on
mount
```

8.4.4 Leveraging Memoization Techniques

Memoization prevents **unnecessary recalculations** and **re-renders**.

1. Use `React.memo` for Pure Components

`React.memo` prevents a component from re-rendering unless its props change.

javascript

```javascript
const ExpensiveComponent = React.memo(({ data
}) => {

  console.log("Re-rendered");

  return <div>{data}</div>;

});
```

2. Use `useMemo` for Caching Expensive Computations

Example: Memoizing Filtered Data

javascript

```javascript
const filteredItems = useMemo(() => {

  return items.filter((item) => item.inStock);

}, [items]);
```

8.4.5 Choosing the Right State Management Approach

Approach	Best For	Example Use Case
Local State	Component-specific state	Form inputs, modals
Context API	Global, low-frequency updates	Theme, authentication
Zustand	Lightweight global state	UI state, small apps
Recoil	Fine-grained reactivity	Global state with computed values
Redux Toolkit	Complex state management	Large-scale applications

When to Use Context vs. Zustand vs. Redux

Scenario	Recommended Approach
Sharing theme settings	Context API
Managing user authentication	Context API or Zustand
Handling UI state (modals, toggles)	Zustand
Complex app state (e.g., e-commerce cart)	Redux Toolkit
Real-time state updates with computed dependencies	Recoil

Chapter 9: Authentication and Authorization

Authentication and authorization are fundamental aspects of modern web applications, ensuring that users can securely access resources based on their identity and roles. In this chapter, we will explore **OAuth and JWT authentication, role-based access control (RBAC), securing pages and routes using middleware**, and **NextAuth.js for seamless authentication**.

By the end of this chapter, you will be able to:

- Implement **OAuth-based authentication** with providers like Google, GitHub, and Facebook.

- Securely **authenticate users with JWT tokens** in a Next.js application.

- Implement **role-based access control (RBAC)** to restrict features based on user roles.

- Secure Next.js **pages and API routes** using middleware.

- Integrate **NextAuth.js** for a flexible authentication solution.

9.1 Implementing OAuth and JWT Authentication

Authentication is a critical component of modern web applications, ensuring that users can securely access their accounts and interact with protected resources. In this section, we will explore two widely used authentication mechanisms:

1. **OAuth Authentication** – A delegated authentication method that allows users to log in using third-party providers such as Google, GitHub, or Facebook.

2. **JWT (JSON Web Token) Authentication** – A stateless, token-based authentication method commonly used in modern web applications.

By the end of this section, you will:

- Understand how **OAuth authentication** works in Next.js.

- Implement **Google OAuth authentication** using NextAuth.js.

- Learn about **JWT authentication** and how to issue and verify tokens.

- Secure Next.js API routes using **JWT-based authentication**.

9.1.1 Understanding OAuth and JWT

What is OAuth?

OAuth 2.0 is an **authorization framework** that allows users to authenticate using an external provider. Instead of storing passwords within your application, OAuth enables **secure authentication** through trusted identity providers like Google, Facebook, or GitHub.

OAuth eliminates the need for users to remember multiple credentials, reducing security risks. After successful authentication, the provider issues an **access token**, which the application uses to retrieve user information.

What is JWT Authentication?

JWT (JSON Web Token) is a compact and self-contained way to **transmit authentication data securely** between a client and a server. JWTs are widely used for authentication because they allow **stateless user sessions** without requiring database lookups on every request.

A **JWT consists of three parts**:

1. **Header** – Specifies the signing algorithm (e.g., HS256).

2. **Payload** – Contains user-related claims (e.g., `id`, `email`, `role`).

3. **Signature** – Ensures that the token is **authentic and unaltered**.

Example JWT Payload:

json

```
{

  "sub": "1234567890",

  "email": "user@example.com",

  "role": "admin",

  "iat": 1710000000,

  "exp": 1710600000
```

```
}
```

JWTs are signed using a secret key, making them **tamper-proof**. The server can verify a token's authenticity without contacting a database, improving performance.

9.1.2 Implementing OAuth Authentication with NextAuth.js

Next.js simplifies OAuth authentication with **NextAuth.js**, a flexible authentication library that supports multiple providers.

Step 1: Install NextAuth.js

sh

```
npm install next-auth
```

Step 2: Set Up Environment Variables

Create a .env.local file in the project root and add:

plaintext

```
GOOGLE_CLIENT_ID=your-google-client-id

GOOGLE_CLIENT_SECRET=your-google-client-
secret

NEXTAUTH_SECRET=your-random-secret-key
```

Replace `your-google-client-id` and `your-google-client-secret` with your credentials from the Google Developer Console.

Generate a random secret for `NEXTAUTH_SECRET` using:

sh

```
openssl rand -base64 32
```

Step 3: Configure NextAuth.js

Create a new API route at `pages/api/auth/[...nextauth].js`:

javascript

```
import NextAuth from "next-auth";

import GoogleProvider from "next-auth/providers/google";

export default NextAuth({
  providers: [
    GoogleProvider({
      clientId: process.env.GOOGLE_CLIENT_ID,
      clientSecret: process.env.GOOGLE_CLIENT_SECRET,
```

```
    }),
  ],
  callbacks: {
    async session({ session, token }) {
      session.user.id = token.sub;
      return session;
    },
  },
});
```

This configures Google OAuth as an authentication provider. The session callback includes the user ID in the session data.

Step 4: Create a Login Button

In components/LoginButton.js:

javascript

```
import { signIn, signOut, useSession } from
"next-auth/react";

export default function LoginButton() {

  const { data: session } = useSession();

  return session ? (
```

```
<div>

  <p>Welcome, {session.user.name}</p>

  <button onClick={() => signOut()}>Sign
Out</button>

  </div>

) : (

  <button                  onClick={()                   =>
signIn("google")}>Sign In with Google</button>

  );

}
```

This button dynamically displays either a **sign-in** or **sign-out** option based on the user's authentication status.

Step 5: Protect a Page

To protect a page and restrict access to authenticated users, wrap the component with NextAuth's useSession hook:

javascript

```
import { useSession } from "next-auth/react";

export default function Dashboard() {

  const { data: session } = useSession();
```

```
  if (!session) {

    return <p>You must be logged in to access
this page.</p>;

  }

  return                          <h1>Welcome,
{session.user.name}</h1>;

}
```

Now, users must be signed in to view the dashboard.

9.1.3 Implementing JWT Authentication in Next.js

While OAuth is excellent for third-party authentication, some applications require **custom authentication** using a **JWT-based system**. This section will guide you through setting up JWT authentication.

Step 1: Install Dependencies

sh

```
npm install jsonwebtoken bcryptjs
```

Step 2: Create a Login API Route

In `pages/api/auth/login.js`:

javascript

```javascript
import jwt from "jsonwebtoken";

import bcrypt from "bcryptjs";

const users = [

  { email: "user@example.com", password:
"$2a$10$hashed_password" }

];

export default async function handler(req,
res) {

  if (req.method !== "POST") return
res.status(405).end();


  const { email, password } = req.body;

  const user = users.find((u) => u.email ===
email);


  if (!user || !bcrypt.compareSync(password,
user.password)) {

    return res.status(401).json({ message:
"Invalid credentials" });

  }
```

```javascript
const token = jwt.sign(

  { email: user.email, role: "user" },

  process.env.JWT_SECRET,

  { expiresIn: "1h" }

);


  res.status(200).json({ token });

}
```

This API route verifies the user's credentials and returns a **JWT** if authentication is successful.

Step 3: Protect API Routes with JWT Middleware

Create `middleware/auth.js`:

javascript

```javascript
import jwt from "jsonwebtoken";

export function authenticateToken(req, res, next) {

  const token = req.headers.authorization?.split(" ")[1];

  if (!token) return res.status(401).json({ message: "Unauthorized" });
```

```javascript
  try {

    req.user         =         jwt.verify(token,
process.env.JWT_SECRET);

    next();

  } catch {

    res.status(403).json({          message:
"Forbidden" });

  }

}
```

This middleware extracts the **JWT token** from the request headers and verifies it.

Step 4: Secure a Protected API Route

Modify an API route to use the middleware:

javascript

```javascript
import   {   authenticateToken   }   from
"../../middleware/auth";

export default function handler(req, res) {

  authenticateToken(req, res, () => {

    res.status(200).json({          message:
"Protected data", user: req.user });

  });
```

```
}
```

Now, only authenticated users with a valid JWT can access this API.

9.2 Role-Based Access Control in Next.js

Role-Based Access Control (RBAC) is a security approach that restricts access to specific parts of an application based on a user's role. Implementing RBAC in a Next.js application ensures that only authorized users can perform certain actions or view protected content.

By the end of this section, you will:

- Understand **RBAC and its importance** in web applications.

- Implement **role-based authentication using NextAuth.js**.

- Secure **API routes and UI components** based on user roles.

- Learn **best practices** for managing roles in a Next.js application.

9.2.1 Understanding Role-Based Access Control

RBAC is a method of **assigning permissions based on predefined roles**, rather than managing permissions individually for each user.

Key Concepts of RBAC

- **Roles** – Defined user categories (e.g., "admin", "editor", "user").

- **Permissions** – Allowed actions based on a user's role (e.g., "edit posts", "delete users").

- **Role Assignments** – Mapping users to specific roles.

Example of Role Permissions

Role	View Pages	Edit Content	Delete Users	Manage Users
User	Yes	No	NO	NO
Editor	Yes	Yes	NO	NO
Admin	Yes	Yes	Yes	Yes

In this model:

- **Users** can only view pages.
- **Editors** can edit content but cannot manage users.
- **Admins** have full control.

9.2.2 Implementing RBAC in Next.js

Step 1: Extend User Roles in NextAuth.js

Modify `pages/api/auth/[...nextauth].js` to include roles in the session:

javascript

```
import NextAuth from "next-auth";

import GoogleProvider from "next-auth/providers/google";

export default NextAuth({

  providers: [

    GoogleProvider({

      clientId: process.env.GOOGLE_CLIENT_ID,

      clientSecret:
process.env.GOOGLE_CLIENT_SECRET,

    }),

  ],

  callbacks: {

    async jwt({ token }) {

      // Assign role based on user email (for
demo purposes)

      if (token.email === "admin@example.com")
{
```

```
      token.role = "admin";

    } else {

      token.role = "user";

    }

    return token;

    },

    async session({ session, token }) {

      session.user.role = token.role;

      return session;

    },

  },

});
```

Explanation:

- The `jwt` callback assigns a role to the user.

- The `session` callback ensures the role is available in the session data.

Step 2: Create a Role-Based Authorization Hook

To easily check user roles throughout the application, create a utility hook:

`hooks/useRole.js`

javascript

```
import { useSession } from "next-auth/react";

export function useRole(requiredRole) {

  const { data: session } = useSession();

    if (!session) return false; // Not
authenticated

    return session.user.role === requiredRole;

}
```

Usage:

- `useRole("admin")` returns `true` if the user is an admin.

- If the user is **not authenticated**, it returns `false`.

Step 3: Protect UI Components Based on Roles

Restricting Admin Dashboard

Modify `pages/admin.js` to restrict access:

javascript

```
import { useRole } from "../hooks/useRole";
```

```javascript
export default function AdminDashboard() {

  const isAdmin = useRole("admin");


  if (!isAdmin) {

    return <p>Access Denied</p>;

  }

  return <h1>Admin Dashboard</h1>;

}
```

Now, only **admins** can view this page.

Step 4: Protect API Routes Based on Roles

To prevent unauthorized users from accessing certain API endpoints, create a **middleware for RBAC**:

middleware/roleAuth.js

javascript

```javascript
import { getSession } from "next-auth/react";

export async function requireRole(req, res,
next, requiredRole) {

  const session = await getSession({ req });

  if (!session || session.user.role !==
requiredRole) {
```

268

```javascript
    return res.status(403).json({ message:
"Forbidden" });
  }


  next();

}
```

Now, apply this middleware to an API route:

`pages/api/admin-data.js`

javascript

```javascript
import { requireRole } from
"../../middleware/roleAuth";

export default async function handler(req,
res) {

  await requireRole(req, res, () => {

    res.status(200).json({ message: "Admin
Data Access Granted" });

  }, "admin");

}
```

Explanation:

- Only users with the **admin role** can access this API.
- Unauthorized users receive a **403 Forbidden** response.

9.2.3 Implementing Multi-Role Permissions

For applications with multiple roles (e.g., editor, admin, user), modify useRole.js:

Enhanced useRole.js for Multiple Roles

javascript

```javascript
export function useRole(requiredRoles) {

  const { data: session } = useSession();

  if (!session) return false; // Not
authenticated

  return
requiredRoles.includes(session.user.role);

}
```

Usage:

- useRole(["admin", "editor"]) allows **both admins and editors**.
- useRole(["user"]) restricts to **regular users**.

Now, update admin.js to allow **both admins and editors**:

javascript

```
const    canAccess    =    useRole(["admin",
"editor"]);

if (!canAccess) {

  return <p>Access Denied</p>;

}
```

9.2.4 Best Practices for Role-Based Access Control

1. **Use Middleware for API Protection** – Ensure API routes check user roles to prevent unauthorized access.

2. **Restrict UI Components** – Hide or disable UI elements that users should not access.

3. **Define Roles Clearly** – Avoid unnecessary roles and ensure permissions are well-defined.

4. **Store Roles Securely** – Do not store user roles in local storage or client-side cookies. Use JWTs or NextAuth sessions.

5. **Regularly Review Permissions** – As your application grows, periodically review and update roles.

9.3 Securing Pages and Routes with Middleware

Middleware in Next.js allows you to **secure pages, API routes, and assets** by intercepting requests before they reach the server or the client.

It provides a powerful way to enforce authentication, authorization, and other security policies at the routing level.

By the end of this section, you will:

- Understand **how middleware works in Next.js**.

- Implement **authentication checks** to protect pages and routes.

- Enforce **role-based access control (RBAC) in middleware**.

- Secure API endpoints with **server-side middleware logic**.

- Learn **best practices for Next.js middleware security**.

9.3.1 Understanding Middleware in Next.js

What Is Middleware?

Middleware is a function that runs **before a request completes**, allowing you to **modify the request or response, redirect users, or deny access** before rendering a page. It is useful for:

- **Authentication enforcement** – Ensuring only logged-in users access certain pages.

- **Role-based authorization** – Restricting routes based on user roles (e.g., admin vs. user).

- **Logging and analytics** – Capturing request data for analytics or debugging.

- **Rate limiting** – Preventing excessive requests from a single user or IP.

How Middleware Works in Next.js 15

Next.js middleware runs in the **Edge Runtime**, meaning it executes **before the request reaches the server or frontend application**. It is defined in the `middleware.js` or `middleware.ts` file at the root of the Next.js project.

Key Features of Next.js Middleware:

- Runs on **Edge Runtime** (fast execution, low latency).

- Intercepts requests **before they reach a page or API**.

- Supports **redirects, rewrites, and response modifications**.

- Can be used **globally or scoped to specific routes**.

9.3.2 Implementing Authentication Middleware

Step 1: Creating Middleware for Authentication

Create a `middleware.js` file at the root of your project:

javascript

```javascript
import { NextResponse } from "next/server";

import { getToken } from "next-auth/jwt";

export async function middleware(req) {

  const token = await getToken({ req, secret:
process.env.NEXTAUTH_SECRET });


  // Define protected routes

  const protectedRoutes = ["/dashboard",
"/profile", "/settings"];

  if
(protectedRoutes.includes(req.nextUrl.pathnam
e)) {

    if (!token) {

      return          NextResponse.redirect(new
URL("/login", req.url));

    }

  }


  return NextResponse.next();

}
```

```
export const config = {

  matcher:      ["/dashboard",      "/profile",
"/settings"], // Apply to these routes

};
```

Explanation:

- The middleware checks if a user has a valid **NextAuth session token**.

- If the user **is not authenticated**, they are **redirected to the login page**.

- The `matcher` property ensures the middleware only runs on specific pages.

Step 2: Testing Authentication Middleware

- Try accessing `/dashboard` **without logging in** – You should be redirected to `/login`.

- After logging in, visit `/dashboard` again – You should now have access.

9.3.3 Role-Based Authorization in Middleware

To **enforce role-based access control (RBAC)**, modify the middleware to check **user roles** before allowing access.

Step 1: Update Middleware to Check User Roles

Modify `middleware.js` to restrict access based on roles:

javascript

```javascript
import { NextResponse } from "next/server";

import { getToken } from "next-auth/jwt";

export async function middleware(req) {

  const token = await getToken({ req, secret:
process.env.NEXTAUTH_SECRET });

  const adminRoutes = ["/admin", "/manage-
users"];

  const editorRoutes = ["/edit-content"];

  if (!token) {

    return          NextResponse.redirect(new
URL("/login", req.url));

  }

  // Restrict access to admin routes
```

```
  if
(adminRoutes.includes(req.nextUrl.pathname)
&& token.role !== "admin") {

    return            NextResponse.redirect(new
URL("/unauthorized", req.url));

  }

  // Restrict access to editor routes

  if
(editorRoutes.includes(req.nextUrl.pathname)
&& !["admin", "editor"].includes(token.role))
{

    return            NextResponse.redirect(new
URL("/unauthorized", req.url));

  }

  return NextResponse.next();

}

export const config = {

  matcher: ["/admin", "/manage-users", "/edit-
content"], // Apply to these routes

};
```

Explanation:

- Admin pages (/admin, /manage-users) are restricted **to admins only**.

- Editor pages (/edit-content) allow **both admins and editors**.

- Unauthorized users are **redirected to** /unauthorized.

Step 2: Handling Unauthorized Access

Create an unauthorized.js page in pages/:

javascript

```
export default function Unauthorized() {

  return (

    <div>

      <h1>Access Denied</h1>

      <p>You do not have permission to access this page.</p>

    </div>

  );

}
```

Step 3: Testing Role-Based Middleware

1. Try visiting /admin as a **non-admin user** – You should be redirected to /unauthorized.

2. Log in as an **editor** and visit /edit-content – You should have access.

3. Log in as an **admin** and visit /manage-users – You should have access.

9.3.4 Securing API Routes with Middleware

Middleware can also **protect API routes**, ensuring only authorized users can make requests.

Step 1: Create API Middleware

Modify middleware.js to apply authentication to API routes:

javascript

```
export async function middleware(req) {

  const token = await getToken({ req, secret:
process.env.NEXTAUTH_SECRET });


  if
(req.nextUrl.pathname.startsWith("/api/admin"
)) {

    if (!token || token.role !== "admin") {
```

```
      return    NextResponse.json({    message:
"Forbidden" }, { status: 403 });

    }

  }

  return NextResponse.next();

}

export const config = {

  matcher: ["/api/admin/:path*"], // Apply to
all admin API routes

};
```

Step 2: Creating a Protected API Route

In pages/api/admin/data.js, create a restricted API route:

javascript

```
export default function handler(req, res) {

  res.status(200).json({ message: "Admin Data
Access Granted" });

}
```

Step 3: Testing API Route Security

1. Try accessing /api/admin/data **without logging in** –
   You should get a 403 Forbidden response.

280

2. Log in as an **admin** and access `/api/admin/data` – You
   should receive a success response.

9.3.5 Best Practices for Securing Pages and Routes

1. **Use Middleware for Centralized Security** – Implement
   authentication and authorization checks at the routing level to
   avoid redundant logic in pages and APIs.

2. **Limit Public Exposure** – Only expose public pages, keeping all
   sensitive routes protected by middleware.

3. **Apply Role-Based Access at Multiple Layers** – Validate user
   roles in both middleware and server-side API handlers.

4. **Redirect Unauthorized Users Gracefully** – Use clear
   messages and proper redirections (`/login` for authentication,
   `/unauthorized` for authorization failures).

5. **Test Security Regularly** – Validate middleware behavior by
   simulating different user roles and testing unauthorized access
   attempts.

9.4 Using NextAuth.js for Seamless Authentication

NextAuth.js is a powerful authentication library designed specifically
for **Next.js applications**, enabling seamless integration with various
authentication providers, including **OAuth (Google, GitHub,**

Facebook, etc.), email/password, and credentials-based authentication.

By the end of this section, you will:

- Understand **how NextAuth.js works** in Next.js 15.
- Set up **NextAuth.js for authentication** in a Next.js application.
- Implement **OAuth authentication** using Google as an example.
- Secure **API routes and pages** using session-based authentication.
- Learn **best practices for managing authentication in Next.js applications**.

9.4.1 Introduction to NextAuth.js

Why Use NextAuth.js?

NextAuth.js simplifies authentication in Next.js applications by providing:

- **Built-in support for multiple authentication providers** (OAuth, email, credentials, etc.).

- **Session management** with automatic handling of authentication state.

- **Secure, server-side authentication** without exposing sensitive credentials to the client.

- **Middleware integration** for protecting pages and routes.

- **Easy customization** to fit different authentication flows.

How NextAuth.js Works

NextAuth.js consists of **three key components**:

1. **API Route** (`/api/auth/[...nextauth]`) – The Next.js API route that handles authentication.

2. **Providers** – The authentication methods used (Google, GitHub, email, credentials, etc.).

3. **Session Management** – NextAuth.js maintains the user session on the server and client.

When a user logs in, NextAuth.js:

- **Authenticates the user** using the selected provider.

- **Creates a session** and stores it securely using cookies or JWT.

- **Makes session data available** to pages and API routes.

9.4.2 Installing and Configuring NextAuth.js

Step 1: Install NextAuth.js

Run the following command to install NextAuth.js in your Next.js project:

sh

```sh
npm install next-auth
```

Step 2: Create API Route for NextAuth.js

In Next.js, authentication is handled via an API route at `/api/auth/[...nextauth].js`. Create the file:

sh

```sh
mkdir -p pages/api/auth
touch pages/api/auth/[...nextauth].js
```

Now, open `pages/api/auth/[...nextauth].js` and set up NextAuth.js:

javascript

```javascript
import NextAuth from "next-auth";
import GoogleProvider from "next-auth/providers/google";
```

```
export default NextAuth({

  providers: [

    GoogleProvider({

      clientId: process.env.GOOGLE_CLIENT_ID,

      clientSecret:
process.env.GOOGLE_CLIENT_SECRET,

    }),

  ],

  secret: process.env.NEXTAUTH_SECRET,

});
```

Step 3: Set Up Environment Variables

Create a `.env.local` file in your project root and add the following variables:

env

```
GOOGLE_CLIENT_ID=your_google_client_id

GOOGLE_CLIENT_SECRET=your_google_client_secre
t

NEXTAUTH_SECRET=your_random_secret
```

Replace `your_google_client_id` and `your_google_client_secret` with credentials from the **Google Developer Console**.

Step 4: Restart Your Next.js Server

After adding environment variables, restart your server:

sh

```
npm run dev
```

Now, visit `/api/auth/signin` in your browser. You should see the Google authentication page.

9.4.3 Implementing Authentication in the Frontend

Step 1: Set Up the Authentication Context

NextAuth.js provides a `useSession` hook to manage authentication state. Wrap your application in the `SessionProvider` component in `_app.js`:

javascript

```
import { SessionProvider } from "next-
auth/react";

export default function MyApp({ Component,
pageProps }) {

  return (
```

```
    <SessionProvider
session={pageProps.session}>

      <Component {...pageProps} />

    </SessionProvider>

  );

}
```

Step 2: Create Login and Logout Buttons

Create a new component components/AuthButtons.js to handle authentication actions:

javascript

```
import { signIn, signOut, useSession } from
"next-auth/react";

export default function AuthButtons() {

  const { data: session } = useSession();

  if (session) {

    return (

      <div>

        <p>Welcome, {session.user.name}!</p>

        <button onClick={() => signOut()}>Sign
Out</button>
```

```
      </div>

    );

  }

  return     <button    onClick={()    =>
signIn("google")}>Sign           In           with
Google</button>;

}
```

Step 3: Add Authentication to the Navbar

Modify your `components/Navbar.js` to include authentication buttons:

javascript

```
import AuthButtons from "./AuthButtons";

export default function Navbar() {

  return (

    <nav>

      <h1>My Next.js App</h1>

      <AuthButtons />

    </nav>

  );
```

```
}
```

9.4.4 Protecting Pages with NextAuth.js

To restrict access to pages, use the useSession hook.

Step 1: Create a Protected Dashboard Page

Create pages/dashboard.js:

javascript

```javascript
import { useSession } from "next-auth/react";

export default function Dashboard() {

  const { data: session } = useSession();

  if (!session) {

    return <p>Access Denied. Please sign in.</p>;

  }

  return <h1>Welcome to the Dashboard, {session.user.name}!</h1>;

}
```

Now, try visiting /dashboard:

- **If not logged in**, it will show "Access Denied"

- **If logged in**, it will display "Welcome to the Dashboard"

9.4.5 Securing API Routes with Authentication

Step 1: Create a Secure API Route

Modify `pages/api/protected.js` to restrict access:

javascript

```javascript
import { getSession } from "next-auth/react";

export default async function handler(req, res) {

  const session = await getSession({ req });

  if (!session) {

    return res.status(401).json({ error: "Unauthorized" });

  }

  res.status(200).json({ message: "Protected data" });

}
```

Step 2: Test the API Route

Try accessing `/api/protected` in your browser or Postman:

- **Without logging in**, it should return: `{ "error": "Unauthorized" }`.

- **After logging in**, it should return: `{ "message": "Protected data" }`.

9.4.6 Best Practices for Authentication in Next.js

1. **Use Environment Variables for Secrets** – Never hardcode client secrets in your code.

2. **Secure API Routes** – Always check user sessions in API routes.

3. **Use Middleware for Global Protection** – Implement authentication middleware to protect multiple pages.

4. **Optimize Session Handling** – Configure session strategies for performance (e.g., JWT for stateless authentication).

5. **Limit OAuth Scopes** – Request only the necessary permissions when using OAuth providers.

Part 4: Performance Optimization and Deployment

Chapter 10: Optimizing Performance in Next.js

Performance optimization is a critical aspect of building **fast, efficient, and scalable** web applications. Next.js provides **built-in features** to enhance performance, including **code splitting, image optimization, caching mechanisms, and server-side optimizations**.

By the end of this chapter, you will:

- Learn how **code splitting and lazy loading** improve page load speed.
- Optimize images using the **next/image** component.
- Improve **Lighthouse performance scores** by addressing key bottlenecks.
- Implement **advanced caching and load balancing strategies** to handle high traffic efficiently.

10.1 Code Splitting and Lazy Loading

In modern web development, delivering high-performance applications is crucial for user engagement and retention. One effective strategy to enhance performance is through **code splitting** and **lazy loading**. These techniques allow developers to load only the necessary code for a page, reducing initial load times and improving the overall user experience. Next.js 15 offers robust support for both code splitting and lazy loading, making it straightforward to implement these optimizations in your applications.

10.1.1 Understanding Code Splitting and Lazy Loading

Code splitting refers to the process of breaking down your code into smaller chunks, which can then be loaded on demand or in parallel. This means that instead of delivering a single, large JavaScript bundle to the client, the application sends only the code required for the current page or feature. This approach significantly reduces the initial load time and bandwidth usage.DEV Community

Lazy loading complements code splitting by deferring the loading of non-essential resources until they are needed. For instance, components that are not immediately visible on the screen, such as modals or complex charts, can be loaded only when the user interacts with a specific feature. This strategy ensures that the initial page loads faster, enhancing the perceived performance of the application.blogs.saurabh-rai.com+1LinkedIn+1

10.1.2 Implementing Dynamic Imports with `next/dynamic`

Next.js provides a powerful utility called `next/dynamic` to facilitate dynamic imports, enabling both code splitting and lazy loading of React components. This function allows you to import components asynchronously, ensuring they are only included in the client-side bundle when required.DhiWise+1web.dev+1

Basic Dynamic Import

To dynamically import a component in Next.js, you can use the `dynamic` function as follows: prateekshawebdesign.com+7DhiWise+7CodeMax+7

jsx

```jsx
import dynamic from 'next/dynamic';

const DynamicComponent = dynamic(() =>
import('../components/MyComponent'));

function Page() {

  return (

    <div>

      <h1>My Page</h1>

      <DynamicComponent />

    </div>

  );

}

export default Page;
```

In this example:

- The MyComponent is not included in the initial JavaScript bundle.Next.js by Vercel - The React Framework

- It is loaded only when DynamicComponent is rendered.
- This reduces the initial load time by deferring the loading of MyComponent until it's needed.Next.js by Vercel - The React Framework+10Next.js by Vercel - The React Framework+10Stack Overflow+10

Adding a Loading Indicator

While the dynamic component is being loaded, it's good practice to display a loading indicator to inform users that content is on the way. You can achieve this by providing a loading component:

jsx

```
import dynamic from 'next/dynamic';

const DynamicComponent = dynamic(() =>
import('../components/MyComponent'), {

  loading: () => <p>Loading...</p>,

});

function Page() {

  return (

    <div>

      <h1>My Page</h1>

      <DynamicComponent />

    </div>

  );

}
export default Page;
```

In this setup:

- The text "Loading..." is displayed while `MyComponent` is being fetched and rendered.

- This enhances the user experience by providing immediate feedback during the loading process.

Disabling Server-Side Rendering

By default, Next.js attempts to render components on the server. However, some components rely on client-side APIs and should only be rendered on the client. To disable server-side rendering for a dynamically imported component, set the `ssr` option to `false`: prateekshawebdesign.com+1CodeMax+1

jsx

```jsx
import dynamic from 'next/dynamic';

const DynamicComponent = dynamic(() =>
import('../components/ClientOnlyComponent'),
{

  ssr: false,

});

function Page() {

  return (

    <div>

      <h1>My Page</h1>
```

```
      <DynamicComponent />

    </div>

  );

}

export default Page;
```

Here:

- `ClientOnlyComponent` will only be rendered on the client side.

- This is useful for components that depend on browser-specific APIs or need access to `window` or `document` objects.

10.1.3 Route-Based Code Splitting

Next.js automatically performs route-based code splitting. Each page in the `pages` directory is code-split into its own JavaScript bundle. When a user navigates to a different route, Next.js loads the corresponding page's code on demand. This default behavior ensures that only the necessary code for the current page is loaded, optimizing the application's   performance.
DhiWise+6web.dev+6CodeMax+6GeeksforGeeks+1Sling Academy+1

10.1.4 Best Practices for Code Splitting and Lazy Loading

To effectively utilize code splitting and lazy loading in Next.js:

1. **Identify Large Dependencies**: Analyze your application to find large dependencies that are not needed immediately. Consider dynamically importing these to reduce the initial bundle size.DEV Community

2. **Use Dynamic Imports for Non-Critical Components**: Components like modals, tooltips, or complex charts that are not essential for the initial render can be loaded dynamically.

3. **Provide Meaningful Loading States**: Always offer users feedback when loading components asynchronously to enhance the user experience.

4. **Test and Monitor Performance**: Regularly test your application's performance using tools like Lighthouse to ensure that code splitting and lazy loading are effectively improving load times.

By implementing these strategies, you can significantly enhance the performance of your Next.js applications, leading to faster load times and a more responsive user experience.

10.2 Image Optimization with next/image

Images play a crucial role in modern web applications, but they can also be one of the biggest contributors to slow page load times and poor performance. To address this, Next.js provides the `next/image` component, a powerful built-in solution for automatic image optimization. This feature helps improve loading times, reduce bandwidth usage, and enhance the overall user experience by delivering responsive, optimized images.

10.2.1 Why Use `next/image`?

Unlike standard HTML `<img>` tags or traditional image-handling methods, `next/image` provides several key advantages:

- **Automatic Optimization**: Images are automatically resized, compressed, and served in modern formats like WebP to improve performance.

- **Responsive Loading**: The component adjusts image sizes dynamically based on the device's screen size and resolution.

- **Lazy Loading by Default**: Images load only when they are needed, reducing unnecessary network requests.

- **Built-in Caching**: Optimized images are cached to minimize server load and improve performance.

- **Support for External and Remote Images**: The component allows fetching images from external sources efficiently.

By leveraging these features, developers can enhance page speed while maintaining high-quality visuals.

10.2.2 Getting Started with `next/image`

To use the `next/image` component, first ensure that your Next.js 15 project is set up. The component is available by default in Next.js and does not require additional installation.

Basic Usage

To render an optimized image using `next/image`, import the component and specify the image source:

jsx

```
import Image from 'next/image';

function HomePage() {

  return (

    <div>

      <h1>Welcome to My Website</h1>

      <Image

        src="/images/sample.jpg"

        alt="Sample Image"

        width={600}

        height={400}

      />
```

```
      </div>

  );

}

export default HomePage;
```

Explanation:

- The src attribute specifies the image source.
- The alt attribute provides alternative text for accessibility.
- The width and height attributes define the image dimensions.
- Next.js optimizes the image automatically, serving the most efficient format.

Lazy Loading by Default

By default, next/image enables lazy loading, meaning images are only loaded when they enter the viewport. This improves performance by reducing the number of initial network requests.

10.2.3 Responsive Images with next/image

To make images responsive, use the fill attribute instead of setting fixed width and height values:

jsx

```
import Image from 'next/image';

function ResponsiveImage() {
```

```
  return (

    <div style={{ position: 'relative', width:
'100%', height: '400px' }}>

      <Image

        src="/images/responsive.jpg"

        alt="Responsive Image"

        fill

        style={{ objectFit: 'cover' }}

      />

    </div>

  );

}

export default ResponsiveImage;
```

Explanation:

- The `fill` attribute allows the image to adapt to the parent container's dimensions.

- The `style` property with `objectFit: 'cover'` ensures the image fills the container without distortion.

10.2.4 Handling External Images

By default, Next.js restricts images to local assets for security and performance reasons. To load images from external sources, update the `next.config.js` file:

javascript

```javascript
module.exports = {
  images: {
    remotePatterns: [
      {
        protocol: 'https',
        hostname: 'example.com',
      },
    ],
  },
};
```

Then, use `next/image` to render an image from the external domain:

jsx

```jsx
import Image from 'next/image';
function ExternalImage() {
  return (
```

```
  <Image

    src="https://example.com/sample.jpg"

    alt="External Image"

    width={500}

    height={300}

  />

  );

}

export default ExternalImage;
```

Key Points:

- The `remotePatterns` configuration allows fetching images from external domains.

- This setup ensures external images benefit from Next.js's optimization features.

10.2.5 Using the `priority` Attribute for Above-the-Fold Images

By default, `next/image` loads images lazily. However, for above-the-fold content (e.g., hero images), it is beneficial to prioritize loading:

jsx

```jsx
import Image from 'next/image';

function HeroImage() {

  return (

    <Image

      src="/images/hero.jpg"

      alt="Hero Section"

      width={1200}

      height={600}

      priority

    />

  );

}


export default HeroImage;
```

Explanation:

- The `priority` attribute ensures the image loads immediately, improving perceived performance.

- This is ideal for key images that should appear as soon as the page loads.

10.2.6 Optimizing Performance with Proper Image Formats

Next.js automatically serves optimized image formats such as WebP when supported. However, you can explicitly specify formats using the formats attribute:

jsx

```
import Image from 'next/image';

function OptimizedImage() {

  return (

    <Image

      src="/images/optimized.jpg"

      alt="Optimized Image"

      width={800}

      height={500}

      formats={['image/webp', 'image/jpeg']}

    />

  );
```

```
}
export default OptimizedImage;
```

Key Benefits:

- WebP format provides superior compression and quality.

- The browser selects the most appropriate format for better performance.

10.2.7 Best Practices for Image Optimization in Next.js

To maximize performance and efficiency when working with `next/image`:

1. **Use the Smallest Necessary Image Size**

   - Avoid using excessively large images. Resize images before uploading when possible.

2. **Leverage Automatic Format Conversion**

   - Let Next.js serve WebP images where supported for better compression.

3. **Prioritize Critical Images**

o Use the `priority` attribute for images above the fold to ensure faster loading.

4. **Avoid Unnecessary Remote Image Requests**

   o Whenever possible, host images locally for faster and more reliable performance.

5. **Use CDN for Global Image Distribution**

   o Consider hosting images on a CDN to reduce latency for users worldwide.

10.3 Improving Lighthouse Performance Scores

Website performance is a critical factor in user experience, SEO rankings, and overall application efficiency. Google Lighthouse is a powerful open-source tool that helps developers analyze and improve their web applications by providing detailed performance audits. Next.js 15, with its built-in optimizations, makes it easier to achieve high Lighthouse scores, but additional strategies can further enhance your application's performance.

In this section, we will explore how to use Lighthouse effectively, interpret its audit results, and implement best practices to improve key performance metrics.

10.3.1 Understanding Lighthouse Metrics

Lighthouse evaluates web pages based on five primary categories:

1. **Performance** – Measures load time, interactivity, and responsiveness.

2. **Accessibility** – Evaluates adherence to web accessibility standards.

3. **Best Practices** – Checks for security vulnerabilities and development standards.

4. **SEO** – Assesses search engine optimization factors.

5. **Progressive Web App (PWA)** – Ensures compliance with PWA requirements.

For Next.js applications, performance is the most critical metric, directly influencing user experience and search engine rankings.

Key Performance Metrics:

- **First Contentful Paint (FCP):** Time taken for the first visible content to load.

- **Largest Contentful Paint (LCP):** Time taken for the largest visible element to load.

- **Cumulative Layout Shift (CLS):** Measures unexpected layout shifts during page load.

- **Time to Interactive (TTI):** Time required for the page to become fully interactive.

- **Total Blocking Time (TBT):** Measures input delay caused by JavaScript execution.

Improving these metrics ensures a fast, smooth, and responsive user experience.

10.3.2 Running a Lighthouse Audit

To generate a Lighthouse report:

Option 1: Using Chrome DevTools

1. Open **Google Chrome**.

2. Press `Ctrl + Shift + I` (or `Cmd + Option + I` on Mac) to open **DevTools**.

3. Navigate to the **Lighthouse** tab.

4. Click **Analyze page load** to generate a report.

Option 2: Using the Lighthouse CLI

Install Lighthouse globally via npm:

sh

```
npm install -g lighthouse
```

Run an audit on a Next.js application:

sh

```
lighthouse https://your-website.com --view
```

This generates a detailed report highlighting areas for improvement.

10.3.3 Optimizing Next.js for Better Lighthouse Scores

1. Improve First Contentful Paint (FCP) and Largest Contentful Paint (LCP)

- Use `next/image` for optimized image loading.

- Minimize render-blocking CSS and JavaScript.

- Enable automatic static optimization for pages where possible.

- Use a Content Delivery Network (CDN) to serve static assets.

Example: Optimized Image Loading

jsx

```
import Image from 'next/image';

function OptimizedHero() {
  return (
```

```
<Image

  src="/hero.jpg"

  alt="Hero Image"

  width={1200}

  height={600}

  priority

/>

  );

}

export default OptimizedHero;
```

Using `priority` ensures the hero image loads early, improving LCP.

2. Reduce JavaScript Execution Time

- **Use code splitting with `React.lazy` and `next/dynamic`.**

- **Remove unused JavaScript and dependencies.**

- **Optimize third-party scripts by deferring or asynchronously loading them.**

Example: Dynamic Import with `next/dynamic`

jsx

```jsx
import dynamic from 'next/dynamic';

const HeavyComponent = dynamic(() =>
import('../components/HeavyComponent'), {

  ssr: false,

});

function HomePage() {

 return (

    <div>

      <h1>Home Page</h1>

      <HeavyComponent />

    </div>

  );

}


export default HomePage;
```

This prevents large components from loading until needed, improving TTI.

3. Optimize Cumulative Layout Shift (CLS)

- **Specify dimensions for images and iframes to prevent reflow.**

- **Avoid inserting dynamic content above existing content.**

- **Use `font-display: swap;` for faster font rendering.**

Example: Preventing Image Layout Shift

jsx

```
<Image
  src="/banner.jpg"
  alt="Banner"
  width={1000}
  height={500}
  layout="intrinsic"
/>
```

Setting explicit width and height prevents CLS issues.

4. Improve Time to Interactive (TTI) and Total Blocking Time (TBT)

- **Defer non-essential scripts.**

- **Minimize large JavaScript bundles.**

- **Use Next.js API routes instead of client-side API calls.**

Example: Deferring Third-Party Scripts

jsx

```jsx
import Script from 'next/script';

function Analytics() {

  return (

    <Script

      src="https://example.com/analytics.js"

      strategy="lazyOnload"

    />

  );

}

export default Analytics;
```

Using `lazyOnload` prevents third-party scripts from blocking page interactivity.

5. Enable Next.js Caching Strategies

- Use `getStaticProps` for static content.

- Use `getServerSideProps` only when dynamic content is necessary.

- Leverage Next.js middleware for caching API responses.

Example: Static Site Generation

jsx

```jsx
export async function getStaticProps() {

  const        res        =        await
fetch('https://api.example.com/data');

  const data = await res.json();

  return {

    props: { data },

    revalidate: 60, // Regenerate the page
every 60 seconds

  };

}

function Page({ data }) {

  return   <pre>{JSON.stringify(data,   null,
2)}</pre>;
```

```
}
```

```
export default Page;
```

This ensures fast performance by generating static pages and revalidating them periodically.

10.3.4 Leveraging Next.js Middleware for Performance

Middleware can optimize performance by handling redirections, caching responses, and reducing unnecessary API calls.

Example: Middleware for API Caching

javascript

```javascript
import { NextResponse } from 'next/server';

export function middleware(req) {

  const cacheControlHeader = 'public, s-maxage=600, stale-while-revalidate=300';

  const response = NextResponse.next();

  response.headers.set('Cache-Control', cacheControlHeader);

  return response;
```

```
}
```

This caches API responses for 10 minutes, reducing unnecessary re-fetching.

10.3.5 Measuring Progress and Continuous Optimization

1. **Run Lighthouse audits regularly** to track improvements.

2. **Monitor Core Web Vitals** using Google PageSpeed Insights.

3. **Optimize performance for mobile-first** experiences.

4. **Use Next.js analytics tools** to measure real-world performance.

10.4 Advanced Caching and Load Balancing Strategies

Optimizing performance in Next.js applications requires advanced caching and load balancing strategies. These techniques help reduce server load, improve response times, and ensure scalability under high traffic conditions. By leveraging Next.js caching mechanisms, Content Delivery Networks (CDNs), and efficient load balancing, developers can build robust, high-performance applications.

In this section, we will explore advanced caching strategies, including static generation, server-side caching, API response caching, and Edge caching. We will also discuss load balancing strategies for distributing traffic efficiently across multiple servers.

10.4.1 Understanding Caching in Next.js

Caching is a critical aspect of performance optimization, reducing the need for redundant computations and database queries. Next.js provides multiple caching mechanisms:

1. **Static Generation (SSG) Caching** – Pre-renders pages at build time.

2. **Incremental Static Regeneration (ISR)** – Updates static pages at runtime.

3. **Server-Side Rendering (SSR) Caching** – Caches server-rendered responses.

4. **API Response Caching** – Stores API responses to reduce redundant requests.

5. **Edge Caching** – Uses CDNs and edge functions to serve content closer to users.

Each caching strategy serves a unique purpose, and combining them effectively can significantly improve performance.

10.4.2 Static Generation and Incremental Static Regeneration

Static Generation (SSG)

Next.js pre-renders pages at build time, caching them as static files. This is ideal for content that does not change frequently.

Example: Static Generation with `getStaticProps`

javascript

```javascript
export async function getStaticProps() {

  const       response       =       await
fetch('https://api.example.com/posts');

  const posts = await response.json();

  return {

    props: { posts },

  };

}

function Blog({ posts }) {

  return (

    <div>

      <h1>Blog Posts</h1>

      <ul>

        {posts.map((post) => (

          <li key={post.id}>{post.title}</li>

        ))}
```

```
      </ul>

    </div>

  );

}

export default Blog;
```

The page is built once and served statically, reducing server processing time.

Incremental Static Regeneration (ISR)

ISR allows Next.js to regenerate static pages in the background, ensuring fresh content without rebuilding the entire application.

Example: ISR Implementation

javascript

```
export async function getStaticProps() {

  const         response         =         await
fetch('https://api.example.com/posts');

  const posts = await response.json();

  return {

    props: { posts },

    revalidate: 60, // Regenerates the page
every 60 seconds

  };
```

```
}
```

This ensures pages remain updated while maintaining static performance benefits.

10.4.3 Server-Side Caching for Dynamic Content

For pages requiring dynamic content, caching can be implemented at the server level using HTTP headers or in-memory stores like Redis.

Implementing HTTP Cache Headers

Next.js API routes can set cache-control headers to store responses in intermediary caches.

Example: Caching API Responses

javascript

```javascript
export default async function handler(req, res) {

  res.setHeader('Cache-Control', 's-maxage=600, stale-while-revalidate=300');

  const response = await fetch('https://api.example.com/data');

  const data = await response.json();

  res.status(200).json(data);

}
```

- `s-maxage=600`: Caches the response for 10 minutes.

- `stale-while-revalidate=300`: Serves stale data while revalidating in the background.

Using Redis for Caching API Responses

Redis is a high-performance in-memory database that can store frequently accessed data.

Example: Implementing Redis Caching

javascript

```javascript
import Redis from 'ioredis';

const redis = new Redis(process.env.REDIS_URL);

export default async function handler(req, res) {

  const cacheKey = 'api:data';

  const cachedData = await redis.get(cacheKey);

  if (cachedData) {

    return res.status(200).json(JSON.parse(cachedData));

  }
```

```javascript
  const          response          =          await
fetch('https://api.example.com/data');

  const data = await response.json();

  await                    redis.set(cacheKey,
JSON.stringify(data), 'EX', 600); // Cache for
10 minutes

  res.status(200).json(data);

}
```

Using Redis significantly reduces API response times and database queries.

10.4.4 Leveraging Edge Caching for Performance

Edge caching moves content closer to users by storing it in geographically distributed data centers. This reduces latency and improves page load times.

Implementing Edge Middleware in Next.js

Edge middleware allows processing requests at the CDN level before they reach the origin server.

Example: Edge Caching with Next.js Middleware

javascript

```javascript
import { NextResponse } from 'next/server';

export function middleware(req) {
```

```
const response = NextResponse.next();

response.headers.set('Cache-Control',
'public,       max-age=300,       stale-while-
revalidate=150');

return response;

}
```

This caches responses for five minutes, serving stale data while refreshing in the background.

Using CDNs for Static Content

Next.js integrates seamlessly with CDNs like **Vercel Edge Network, Cloudflare, and AWS CloudFront** for distributing static assets globally.

Steps to Use a CDN:

1. **Deploy on Vercel** (automatically uses Edge caching).

2. **Configure Cloudflare or AWS CloudFront** for static asset caching.

3. **Use `next/image` with a CDN** for optimized image delivery.

10.4.5 Load Balancing Strategies for Scalability

Load balancing distributes incoming traffic across multiple servers, ensuring high availability and resilience under heavy traffic loads.

Types of Load Balancing:

1. **Round Robin** – Distributes requests sequentially across servers.

2. **Least Connections** – Sends requests to the server with the fewest active connections.

3. **Geolocation-Based Routing** – Directs users to the nearest data center.

Implementing Load Balancing with Nginx

Nginx can be used as a reverse proxy to distribute traffic across multiple Next.js instances.

Example: Nginx Load Balancing Configuration

nginx

```
upstream nextjs_servers {
    server 192.168.1.101:3000;
    server 192.168.1.102:3000;
    server 192.168.1.103:3000;
}
server {
    listen 80;
    location / {
```

```
        proxy_pass http://nextjs_servers;

        proxy_set_header Host $host;

        proxy_set_header            X-Real-IP
$remote_addr;

        proxy_set_header       X-Forwarded-For
$proxy_add_x_forwarded_for;

    }

}
```

This configuration distributes traffic across three Next.js instances.

Load Balancing with Kubernetes

Kubernetes provides scalable load balancing using `Ingress` controllers.

Example: Kubernetes Ingress Configuration

yaml

```yaml
apiVersion: networking.k8s.io/v1

kind: Ingress

metadata:

  name: nextjs-ingress

spec:

  rules:

    - host: example.com
```

```yaml
http:
  paths:
    - path: /
      pathType: Prefix
      backend:
        service:
          name: nextjs-service
          port:
            number: 3000
```

This routes incoming traffic to a Next.js service running on Kubernetes.

Chapter 11: Deploying Next.js Applications

Deployment is a critical step in building real-world Next.js applications. A well-structured deployment process ensures that applications are performant, scalable, and reliable in production environments. Next.js provides multiple deployment options, from Vercel (the official hosting platform) to cloud providers like AWS, Netlify, and DigitalOcean.

This chapter covers the complete deployment process, including setting up CI/CD pipelines for automated deployments and monitoring applications in production.

11.1 Deploying on Vercel: The Official Platform

Vercel is the official deployment platform for Next.js and is designed to provide a seamless, optimized hosting experience. It offers automatic scaling, serverless functions, and a global content delivery network (CDN) to ensure fast and reliable performance. Deploying a Next.js application on Vercel requires minimal configuration, making it the preferred choice for many developers.

This section covers the entire process of deploying a Next.js application to Vercel, including deploying via the web interface and using the Vercel CLI.

11.1.1 Deploying via Vercel's Web Interface

Vercel provides a direct integration with GitHub, GitLab, and Bitbucket, allowing developers to deploy applications effortlessly.

Step 1: Sign Up on Vercel

1. Navigate to Vercel's official website.

2. Click **Sign Up** and log in using **GitHub, GitLab, or Bitbucket**.

3. Authorize Vercel to access your repository.

Step 2: Import the Next.js Project

1. Click **New Project** in the Vercel dashboard.

2. Select the GitHub repository containing the Next.js application.

3. Click **Import** to start configuring the deployment.

Step 3: Configure Deployment Settings

After importing the repository, configure the deployment settings:

- **Root Directory**: Ensure it points to the Next.js project root.

- **Build Command**: Set to `next build`.

- **Install Command**: Defaults to `npm install` but can be adjusted (`yarn install` or `pnpm install`).

- **Output Directory**: Vercel automatically detects `.next`.

- **Environment Variables**: Add any necessary environment variables used in development and production.

Step 4: Deploy the Application

1. Click **Deploy** to initiate the deployment process.

2. Vercel will install dependencies, build the project, and deploy the application to a unique URL.

3. Once deployed, Vercel provides a preview URL for testing.

Every push to the connected Git repository triggers an automatic deployment, ensuring continuous delivery.

11.1.2 Deploying Using the Vercel CLI

For developers who prefer a command-line approach, the Vercel CLI provides flexibility and control over deployments.

Step 1: Install the Vercel CLI

To install the Vercel CLI globally, run the following command:

sh

```
npm install -g vercel
```

Step 2: Authenticate with Vercel

Log in to Vercel using the CLI:

sh

```
vercel login
```

Follow the authentication process to link the CLI to your Vercel account.

Step 3: Deploy the Next.js Application

Navigate to the root directory of the Next.js project and run:

sh

```
vercel
```

This command will:

- Detect the framework (Next.js).

- Provide options to customize deployment settings.

- Deploy the application and generate a preview URL.

Step 4: Deploy to Production

To deploy directly to the production environment, use:

sh

```
vercel --prod
```

This ensures the deployment is pushed to the production domain.

11.1.3 Configuring Custom Domains

Vercel allows developers to configure custom domains for their applications.

Step 1: Add a Custom Domain

1. Go to the **Vercel Dashboard**.

2. Select the deployed project.

3. Navigate to `Settings → Domains`.

4. Enter the custom domain and click **Add**.

Step 2: Update DNS Records

If the domain is managed by an external provider, update the DNS settings:

- **For root domains (`example.com`)**: Add an A record pointing to Vercel's IP address.

- **For subdomains (`www.example.com`)**: Add a CNAME record pointing to `cname.vercel-dns.com`.

Once configured, Vercel will issue an SSL certificate automatically.

11.1.4 Managing Environment Variables

Environment variables play a crucial role in managing API keys, database credentials, and other sensitive configurations.

Step 1: Define Environment Variables in Vercel

1. Navigate to `Project Settings → Environment Variables`.

2. Click **Add New** and enter the key-value pair.

3. Choose the environment (**Development, Preview, or Production**).

4. Click **Save** and redeploy the application.

Step 2: Access Environment Variables in Next.js

In Next.js, environment variables can be accessed using:

javascript

```
process.env.NEXT_PUBLIC_API_URL
```

For private variables (not exposed to the client):

javascript

```
process.env.DATABASE_SECRET
```

Next.js requires a restart when adding new environment variables locally.

11.1.5 Monitoring Deployments and Performance

Vercel provides built-in tools for monitoring application performance, including analytics, error tracking, and function logs.

Step 1: View Deployment Logs

1. Open the **Vercel Dashboard**.

2. Navigate to **Project → Deployments**.

3. Click on a deployment to view real-time logs.

Step 2: Enable Analytics

1. In **Project Settings**, enable **Vercel Analytics**.

2. Track real-time page views, load times, and performance metrics.

Step 3: Debug Serverless Functions

If using serverless functions, view logs with:

sh

```
vercel logs
```

This command provides detailed logs for debugging API routes and server-side logic.

11.1.6 Rolling Back Deployments

In case of an issue with a new deployment, Vercel allows instant rollbacks.

Step 1: Identify the Previous Deployment

1. Go to `Vercel Dashboard → Deployments`.

2. Locate the previous successful deployment.

Step 2: Revert to the Previous Version

1. Click **Promote to Production** on the selected deployment.

2. The application will revert to the last working version.

This feature ensures quick recovery in case of failed updates.

11.2 Deploying on AWS, Netlify, and DigitalOcean

While Vercel is the official hosting platform for Next.js, many developers prefer to deploy their applications on other cloud platforms like AWS, Netlify, and DigitalOcean. Each platform offers unique advantages, such as greater customization, cost efficiency, and integration with existing cloud services.

This section covers the deployment process for Next.js applications on AWS (using AWS Amplify and EC2), Netlify, and DigitalOcean.

11.2.1 Deploying Next.js on AWS

AWS offers multiple options for deploying Next.js applications, including AWS Amplify for managed hosting and Amazon EC2 for custom deployments.

Deploying with AWS Amplify

AWS Amplify provides a simple way to host Next.js applications with automatic CI/CD pipelines.

Step 1: Set Up AWS Amplify

1. Sign in to the AWS Management Console.

2. Navigate to **AWS Amplify** and click **Get Started**.

Step 2: Connect the Git Repository

1. Click **Host a web app** and choose **GitHub, GitLab, or Bitbucket**.

2. Authorize AWS Amplify to access the repository.

3. Select the repository containing the Next.js application and choose the branch to deploy.

Step 3: Configure Build Settings

AWS Amplify detects the framework and pre-fills the build settings. Ensure the configuration includes:

yaml

```
version: 1
frontend:
  phases:
    preBuild:
      commands:
        - npm install
    build:
      commands:
        - npm run build
  artifacts:
    baseDirectory: .next
    files:
      - '**/*'
  cache:
    paths:
      - node_modules/**/*
```

Step 4: Deploy the Application

1. Click **Save and Deploy**.

2. AWS Amplify builds and deploys the application, providing a unique URL.

Step 5: Configure a Custom Domain (Optional)

1. Navigate to `Amplify Console → Domain Management`.

2. Add a custom domain and update DNS records.

Deploying with AWS EC2

For more control over the server environment, deploying on an Amazon EC2 instance is a viable option.

Step 1: Launch an EC2 Instance

1. Open the EC2 Dashboard.

2. Click **Launch Instance** and choose an Ubuntu or Amazon Linux AMI.

3. Configure the instance, select a security group, and launch the instance.

Step 2: Connect to the Instance

Use SSH to connect to the instance:

sh

```
ssh -i your-key.pem ec2-user@your-ec2-ip
```

340

Step 3: Install Node.js and PM2

Once connected, install Node.js:

sh

```
curl                              -fsSL
https://rpm.nodesource.com/setup_18.x  |  sudo
bash -

sudo yum install -y nodejs
```

Install PM2 for process management:

sh

```
npm install -g pm2
```

Step 4: Deploy the Next.js Application

Clone the repository:

sh
```
git clone https://github.com/your-repo.git

cd your-repo
```

Install dependencies and build the application:

sh

```sh
npm install

npm run build
```

Start the application with PM2:

```sh
pm2 start npm --name "next-app" -- start
```

Step 5: Configure a Reverse Proxy with Nginx

To serve the application on a domain, install and configure Nginx:

sh

```sh
sudo yum install -y nginx

sudo systemctl start nginx
```

Edit the Nginx configuration (`/etc/nginx/nginx.conf`) to include:

nginx

```nginx
server {
    listen 80;
    server_name your-domain.com;
```

```
location / {

    proxy_pass http://localhost:3000;

    proxy_http_version 1.1;

    proxy_set_header                    Upgrade
$http_upgrade;

    proxy_set_header                    Connection
'upgrade';

    proxy_set_header Host $host;

    proxy_cache_bypass $http_upgrade;

}

}
```

Restart Nginx:

sh

```
sudo systemctl restart nginx
```

This setup allows the Next.js application to run behind an Nginx reverse proxy on AWS EC2.

11.2.2 Deploying Next.js on Netlify

Netlify provides a developer-friendly platform for hosting Next.js applications with automatic deployments from Git repositories.

Step 1: Sign Up on Netlify

1. Go to Netlify.

2. Sign in using **GitHub, GitLab, or Bitbucket**.

Step 2: Connect a Git Repository

1. Click **New site from Git**.

2. Select the repository containing the Next.js application.

3. Choose the branch to deploy.

Step 3: Configure Build Settings

Netlify detects Next.js and pre-fills the build settings:

- **Build Command**: `npm run build`

- **Publish Directory**: `.next`

Enable server-side rendering support by adding a `netlify.toml` file:

toml

```
[build]
  command = "npm run build"
  functions = "netlify/functions"
```

```
publish = ".next"


[[headers]]

  for = "/*"

  [headers.values]

    Cache-Control = "public, max-age=31536000,
immutable"
```

Step 4: Deploy the Application

1. Click **Deploy Site**.

2. Once completed, Netlify provides a live URL.

Step 5: Configure a Custom Domain (Optional)

1. Go to **Domain Settings**.

2. Add a custom domain and update DNS records.

Netlify also supports serverless functions for API routes using **Netlify Functions**.

11.2.3 Deploying Next.js on DigitalOcean

DigitalOcean provides a flexible environment for hosting Next.js applications using Droplets or App Platform.

Deploying with DigitalOcean App Platform

Step 1: Create a DigitalOcean Account

Sign up at DigitalOcean and access the App Platform.

Step 2: Create a New App

1. Click **Create → App**.

2. Select the **GitHub repository** containing the Next.js project.

3. Click **Next** to configure the deployment.

Step 3: Set Up Build and Runtime

- **Build Command**: `npm run build`

- **Start Command**: `npm start`

Step 4: Deploy the Application

Click **Deploy** to start the process. DigitalOcean automatically builds and deploys the Next.js application.

Deploying with DigitalOcean Droplet

1. **Create a Droplet** using Ubuntu 22.04.

SSH into the Droplet and install Node.js:

sh
```
curl                           -fsSL
https://deb.nodesource.com/setup_18.x | sudo -
E bash -

sudo apt install -y nodejs
```

Clone the repository and install dependencies:

sh
```
git clone https://github.com/your-repo.git

cd your-repo

npm install

npm run build
```

Start the application with PM2:

sh
```
pm2 start npm --name "next-app" -- start
```

2. **Configure a Reverse Proxy with Nginx** (similar to AWS EC2).

11.3 CI/CD Pipelines for Automated Deployments

Continuous Integration and Continuous Deployment (CI/CD) pipelines automate the process of building, testing, and deploying Next.js applications. Implementing CI/CD ensures that code changes are validated through automated testing and deployed efficiently with minimal manual intervention.

This section covers setting up CI/CD pipelines using **GitHub Actions, GitLab CI/CD, and Jenkins**, providing step-by-step guidance on integrating these pipelines with Next.js applications.

11.3.1 Understanding CI/CD for Next.js

Before diving into implementation, it is essential to understand the core concepts:

- **Continuous Integration (CI)**: Automates testing and building whenever code is pushed to a repository.

- **Continuous Deployment (CD)**: Deploys tested code to a staging or production environment automatically.

- **Continuous Delivery**: Ensures code is always in a deployable state, with deployment requiring manual approval.

CI/CD improves development efficiency by:

- Catching bugs early through automated testing.

- Reducing manual deployment efforts.

- Ensuring faster releases with consistent deployment practices.

11.3.2 Setting Up CI/CD with GitHub Actions

GitHub Actions provides a built-in CI/CD solution to automate testing and deployment directly from a GitHub repository.

Step 1: Create a Workflow File

1. Inside the Next.js project, create a `.github/workflows/deploy.yml` file.

2. Define a workflow for **building and testing** the application:

yaml

```yaml
name: Next.js CI/CD Pipeline

on:

  push:

    branches:

      - main
```

```yaml
  pull_request:
    branches:
      - main
jobs:
  build:
    runs-on: ubuntu-latest
    steps:
      - name: Checkout Code
        uses: actions/checkout@v3
      - name: Setup Node.js
        uses: actions/setup-node@v3
        with:
          node-version: 18
      - name: Install Dependencies
        run: npm install
      - name: Run Tests
        run: npm test
      - name: Build Application
        run: npm run build
```

```
- name: Upload Build Artifacts

  uses: actions/upload-artifact@v3

  with:

    name: next-build

    path: .next
```

This workflow triggers on push and pull_request events to:

- Install dependencies.

- Run tests.

- Build the Next.js application.

- Store the build artifacts for further deployment.

Step 2: Add a Deployment Job

To deploy the Next.js application to **Vercel**, **AWS**, or **DigitalOcean**, update the workflow file:

yaml

```
deploy:

  needs: build

  runs-on: ubuntu-latest

  steps:
```

```
- name: Checkout Code

  uses: actions/checkout@v3

- name: Install Vercel CLI

  run: npm install -g vercel

- name: Deploy to Vercel

  run:      vercel     --token     ${{
secrets.VERCEL_TOKEN }} --prod
```

This deployment step requires a **Vercel API token**, stored as a GitHub **secret** (`VERCEL_TOKEN`).

Step 3: Secure the Pipeline

- Use **GitHub Secrets** to store API keys securely.
- Enable **branch protection rules** to prevent untested code from being merged.
- Run **security audits** with `npm audit` to check for vulnerabilities.

11.3.3 Setting Up CI/CD with GitLab CI/CD

GitLab provides **GitLab CI/CD**, an integrated pipeline system that automates testing and deployment.

Step 1: Create a GitLab CI/CD Configuration File

Inside the Next.js project, create `.gitlab-ci.yml`:

yaml

```yaml
stages:
  - test
  - build
  - deploy

test:
  image: node:18
  stage: test
  script:
    - npm install
    - npm test

build:
  image: node:18
  stage: build
  script:
    - npm install
    - npm run build
```

```
  artifacts:

    paths:

      - .next


deploy:

  image: node:18

  stage: deploy

  only:

    - main

  script:

    - npm install -g vercel

    - vercel --token $VERCEL_TOKEN --prod
```

Step 2: Configure GitLab Environment Variables

1. Navigate to GitLab → Repository → Settings → CI/CD.

2. Under **Variables**, add a new variable:

   ○ **Key**: VERCEL_TOKEN

    ○ **Value**: API token from Vercel.

Step 3: Run the Pipeline

Push changes to GitLab, and the pipeline executes:

1. Runs tests.

2. Builds the Next.js application.

3. Deploys the application using Vercel.

11.3.4 Setting Up CI/CD with Jenkins

Jenkins is a self-hosted automation server that enables customizable CI/CD pipelines.

Step 1: Install Jenkins and Required Plugins

Install Jenkins on a server:

sh

```
wget -q -O - https://pkg.jenkins.io/debian/jenkins.io.key | sudo apt-key add -

sudo sh -c 'echo deb http://pkg.jenkins.io/debian-stable binary/ > /etc/apt/sources.list.d/jenkins.list'
```

```
sudo apt update

sudo apt install jenkins

sudo systemctl start jenkins
```

1.
2. Install the **Node.js Plugin** from the Jenkins Plugin Manager.

Step 2: Create a Jenkinsfile

Inside the Next.js project, create `Jenkinsfile`:

groovy

```groovy
pipeline {
    agent any
    environment {
        VERCEL_TOKEN = credentials('vercel-token')
    }
    stages {
        stage('Checkout Code') {
            steps {
                git branch: 'main', url: 'https://github.com/your-repo.git'
            }
```

```
        }


        stage('Install Dependencies') {

            steps {

                sh 'npm install'

            }

        }


        stage('Run Tests') {

            steps {

                sh 'npm test'

            }

        }


        stage('Build Application') {

            steps {

                sh 'npm run build'

            }

        }
```

```
stage('Deploy to Vercel') {

    steps {

        sh 'npm install -g vercel'

        sh      'vercel      --token
$VERCEL_TOKEN --prod'

    }

  }

 }

}
```

Step 3: Configure Jenkins Pipeline

1. Open Jenkins and create a **new pipeline job**.

2. Under **Pipeline**, select **Pipeline script from SCM**.

3. Choose **Git**, enter the repository URL, and set the branch as
    `main`.

4. Click **Save** and trigger the pipeline.

Jenkins will now automate the build and deployment of the Next.js application.

11.4 Monitoring and Debugging in Production

Deploying a Next.js application to production is just the beginning. To ensure reliability, performance, and stability, developers must implement **monitoring, logging, and debugging strategies**. This section covers **best practices** for tracking application health, identifying performance bottlenecks, and resolving production issues effectively.

11.4.1 The Importance of Monitoring and Debugging

Monitoring and debugging in production help developers:

- **Detect issues early** before they impact users.
- **Track performance metrics** to optimize response times.
- **Analyze error logs** for troubleshooting and debugging.
- **Improve uptime and reliability** with proactive issue resolution.

Monitoring is typically divided into:

1. **Application Monitoring** – Tracks response times, API calls, and errors.

2. **Infrastructure Monitoring** – Observes server health, CPU usage, and memory consumption.

3. **Real User Monitoring (RUM)** – Captures real-time user experiences.

A combination of these approaches ensures a robust **observability strategy**.

11.4.2 Logging and Error Tracking

Logging is the first step in diagnosing production issues. Proper logging helps developers **trace errors, understand performance trends, and identify critical failures**.

Implementing Logging in Next.js

Next.js allows logging on both the **client-side** (browser) and **server-side** (API routes and server-rendered pages).

Client-Side Logging

Use console.log() for debugging in the browser. However, avoid logging **sensitive data** in production.

Example:

javascript

```
useEffect(() => {

  console.log("Page loaded successfully");

}, []);
```

For structured logs, use an external logging service such as **LogRocket** or **Sentry**.

Server-Side Logging

Use `console.log()`, `console.error()`, and `console.warn()` for debugging server-side functions.

Example:

javascript

```javascript
export default function handler(req, res) {

  console.log("Incoming                request:",
req.method, req.url);

  try {

    if (req.method !== "GET") {

      throw new Error("Only GET requests are
allowed");

    }

    res.status(200).json({ message: "Success"
});

  } catch (error) {

    console.error("Error occurred:", error);

    res.status(500).json({ error: "Internal
Server Error" });

  }
```

```
}
```

Best Practices for Logging:

- Use **log levels** (`info`, `warn`, `error`, `debug`).

- Store logs in **external services** like **Logtail**, **Winston**, or **Sentry**.

- Use structured logging with **JSON format** for easy searching.

Integrating Sentry for Error Tracking

Sentry provides real-time error tracking with stack traces and debugging tools.

Step 1: Install Sentry

sh

```sh
npm install @sentry/nextjs
```

Step 2: Configure Sentry in `sentry.server.config.js`

javascript

```javascript
import * as Sentry from "@sentry/nextjs";

Sentry.init({
  dsn: process.env.SENTRY_DSN,
```

```
  tracesSampleRate: 1.0,
});
```

Step 3: Capture Errors in API Routes

javascript

```javascript
import * as Sentry from "@sentry/nextjs";
export default function handler(req, res) {
  try {
    throw new Error("Test error");
  } catch (error) {
    Sentry.captureException(error);
    res.status(500).json({ error:  "Internal
Server Error" });
  }
}
```

Sentry automatically logs errors, providing detailed stack traces for debugging.

11.4.3 Performance Monitoring

Tracking performance ensures that Next.js applications remain fast and responsive.

Using Next.js Built-in Analytics

Next.js provides built-in metrics through the `next/script` module.

Example:

javascript

```javascript
import Script from "next/script";

export default function Home() {

  return (

    <>

      <Script

        src="https://www.google-analytics.com/analytics.js"

        strategy="lazyOnload"

      />

      <h1>Welcome to Next.js</h1>

    </>

  );

}
```

Measuring Web Vitals

Web Vitals measure real-world performance metrics such as **First Contentful Paint (FCP)** and **Largest Contentful Paint (LCP)**.

javascript

```javascript
import { reportWebVitals } from "next/app";

export function reportWebVitals(metric) {

  console.log(metric);

}
```

Use **Google Lighthouse** or **PageSpeed Insights** to analyze performance bottlenecks.

11.4.4 Infrastructure Monitoring

Monitoring the infrastructure ensures **server uptime, load balancing, and database performance**.

Monitoring with Prometheus and Grafana

1. **Install Prometheus** for collecting metrics.

2. **Integrate Next.js with Prometheus** using an API endpoint.

3. **Visualize metrics** in Grafana dashboards.

Example:

javascript

```javascript
import { NextApiRequest, NextApiResponse } from "next";

let requestCount = 0;

export default function handler(req, res) {

  requestCount++;

  res.status(200).json({          requests: requestCount });

}
```

Expose this endpoint in **Prometheus** for tracking API usage.

Using Datadog for Full-Stack Monitoring

1. Sign up at **Datadog** and get an API key.

Install the Datadog agent:

sh

```sh
DD_API_KEY=<your-api-key> bash -c "$(curl -L https://s3.amazonaws.com/dd-agent/scripts/install_script.sh)"
```

2. Configure **APM (Application Performance Monitoring)** in Next.js.

javascript

```
import { tracer } from "dd-trace";

tracer.init({

  service: "nextjs-app",

  env: "production",

});
```

Datadog provides **real-time logs, traces, and monitoring dashboards**.

11.4.5 Debugging Issues in Production

Remote Debugging with Vercel

Vercel provides real-time logs for Next.js applications.

1. Navigate to Vercel Dashboard → Logs.

2. Filter logs by **requests, warnings, and errors**.

3. Use vercel logs <deployment-url> to fetch logs from the terminal.

Debugging Memory Leaks

Memory leaks in Next.js occur when objects persist longer than necessary.

Common causes:

- Unclosed database connections.

- Large objects stored in memory.

- Unoptimized server-side functions.

Fix: Use the **Node.js Heap Snapshot** tool:

sh

```
node --inspect-brk server.js
```

Connect to **Chrome DevTools** and analyze memory usage.

Handling API Failures

Use retries for transient errors:

javascript
```
async function fetchData(url) {

  let retries = 3;

  while (retries > 0) {

    try {

      const response = await fetch(url);
```

```javascript
    if      (!response.ok)      throw      new
Error("Request failed");

    return await response.json();

  } catch (error) {

    console.warn("Retrying request...");

    retries--;

  }

  }

}
```

Implement rate limiting with Redis to prevent overloads:

javascript

```javascript
import rateLimit from "express-rate-limit";

const limiter = rateLimit({

  windowMs: 15 * 60 * 1000,

  max: 100,

});

app.use(limiter);
```

Part 5: Advanced Features and Real-World Projects

Chapter 12: Internationalization (i18n) and Accessibility

Modern web applications must be **accessible to a global audience** and **usable by people with diverse abilities**. This chapter covers **internationalization (i18n)** in Next.js, including **multi-language support and right-to-left (RTL) layouts**, followed by best practices for **building accessible web applications**.

12.1 Setting Up Multi-Language Support in Next.js

Internationalization (**i18n**) enables web applications to support multiple languages, allowing users to interact with content in their preferred language. In this section, we will explore how to implement multi-language support in **Next.js 15**, using built-in **i18n routing** and third-party libraries for dynamic translation management.

12.1.1 Understanding Internationalization in Next.js

Next.js provides built-in **internationalized routing**, which allows applications to:

- Define **multiple locales** for different languages.

- Automatically detect and serve the correct locale based on user preferences.

- Use **localized URLs** (/en, /fr, /es) to differentiate content.

By configuring Next.js correctly, developers can **seamlessly switch languages** while maintaining URL structure and SEO benefits.

12.1.2 Configuring Internationalization in `next.config.js`

To enable internationalization, modify the **Next.js configuration file** (`next.config.js`).

Step 1: Define Supported Locales

javascript

```javascript
module.exports = {
  i18n: {
    locales: ["en", "es", "fr", "de"], //
Supported languages
    defaultLocale: "en", // Default language
  },
};
```

Explanation

- The `locales` array lists all **supported languages** (en, es, fr, de).

- `defaultLocale` defines the **fallback language** when no locale is specified.

Step 2: Create Language-Specific Pages

Next.js will automatically serve content under locale-specific routes. For example, `/about` will have versions like:

- `/en/about` (English)

- `/es/about` (Spanish)

To create **localized pages**, organize them in the `pages` directory:

pgsql

```
pages/
  ├── en/
  │   ├── index.js
  │   ├── about.js
  ├── es/
  │   ├── index.js
  │   ├── about.js
```

Each file should contain **language-specific content**.

Example for `pages/en/index.js`:

javascript

```javascript
export default function Home() {
  return <h1>Welcome to our website</h1>;
}
```

Example for `pages/es/index.js`:

javascript

```javascript
export default function Home() {
  return <h1>Bienvenido a nuestro sitio
web</h1>;
}
```

Now, navigating to `/es/` will display the Spanish version automatically.

12.1.3 Implementing Dynamic Translations with `next-intl`

Manually duplicating pages for each language is inefficient. Instead, use `next-intl` to **load translations dynamically**.

Step 1: Install `next-intl`

sh

```sh
npm install next-intl
```

Step 2: Create a `locales` Folder

Organize translations in **JSON files** inside a `locales` directory:

pgsql

```
locales/
  ├── en.json
  ├── es.json
```

Step 3: Add Translations

`locales/en.json`:

json

```
{
  "welcome": "Welcome to our website",
  "about": "About Us"
}
```

`locales/es.json`:

json

```
{
  "welcome": "Bienvenido a nuestro sitio web",
  "about": "Sobre Nosotros"
}
```

Step 4: Load Translations in Components

Modify `app/layout.js` to use translations dynamically:

javascript

```javascript
import { useTranslations } from "next-intl";

export default function Layout({ children }) {
  const t = useTranslations();

  return (
    <div>
      <h1>{t("welcome")}</h1>
      {children}
    </div>
  );
}
```

Now, the welcome message **automatically updates** based on the user's language.

12.1.4 Language Switching with useRouter

To allow users to **switch languages dynamically**, use next/router.

Step 1: Create a Language Switcher Component

javascript

```javascript
import { useRouter } from "next/router";
import Link from "next/link";

export default function LanguageSwitcher() {
```

```
  const  {  locale,  locales,  asPath  }  =
useRouter();

  return (
    <div>
      {locales.map((lng) => (
        <Link     key={lng}      href={asPath}
locale={lng}>
          <button disabled={lng === locale}>
            {lng.toUpperCase()}
          </button>
        </Link>
      ))}
    </div>
  );
}
```

Explanation

- The useRouter hook retrieves the **current locale and available locales**.

- The Link component updates the URL while maintaining navigation history.

- The button is **disabled for the active language** to prevent redundant clicks.

Step 2: Use the Language Switcher

Place the LanguageSwitcher component in the **main layout**:

javascript
```javascript
import          LanguageSwitcher          from
"./LanguageSwitcher";

export default function Layout({ children }) {
  return (
    <div>
      <LanguageSwitcher />
      {children}
    </div>
  );
}
```

Now, users can dynamically switch between languages using buttons.

12.1.5 Using Server-Side Rendering (SSR) for Translations

When working with **static pages**, translations can be loaded at build time using getStaticProps.

Example

javascript
```javascript
import { useTranslations } from "next-intl";

export async function getStaticProps({ locale
}) {
```

```
  const        messages       =        await
import(`../locales/${locale}.json`);
  return {
    props: {
      messages: messages.default,
    },
  };
}

export default function About() {
  const t = useTranslations();

  return <h1>{t("about")}</h1>;
}
```

Explanation

- getStaticProps loads **translations dynamically** based on the locale.

- import() retrieves the **correct JSON file** at build time.

12.1.6 SEO Optimization for Multi-Language Support

To improve SEO, add **alternate language links** in the <head> section.

Modify pages/_app.js:

```javascript
import Head from "next/head";
import { useRouter } from "next/router";

export default function MyApp({ Component,
pageProps }) {
  const { locale } = useRouter();

  return (
    <>
      <Head>
        <link rel="alternate" hrefLang="en"
href="https://example.com/en" />
        <link rel="alternate" hrefLang="es"
href="https://example.com/es" />
      </Head>
      <Component {...pageProps} />
    </>
  );
}
```

This ensures that **search engines correctly index different language versions**.

12.2 Implementing RTL (Right-to-Left) Support

Many languages, such as Arabic, Hebrew, Persian, and Urdu, are **right-to-left (RTL) languages**. To ensure a seamless user experience, web applications must support **bi-directional layouts** and dynamically adjust **text direction** based on the selected language.

In this section, we will explore:

- Configuring **Next.js** for RTL support.

- Dynamically applying **text direction** using **CSS and JavaScript**.

- Implementing **automatic RTL switching** with **internationalized routing**.

- Using third-party **RTL-friendly UI libraries**.

12.2.1 Understanding RTL vs. LTR Layouts

By default, most web applications use **left-to-right (LTR)** layouts, but RTL languages require adjustments such as:

- **Text alignment:** Right-aligned instead of left-aligned.

- **Navigation structure:** Reversed, with menus and buttons shifting sides.

- **Icons and images:** Some icons (e.g., arrows) need to be mirrored.

- **CSS properties:** `direction: rtl` and `text-align: right` must be applied correctly.

To handle these changes dynamically, Next.js provides a structured approach to switching between LTR and RTL layouts.

12.2.2 Defining RTL Languages in `next.config.js`

First, update the `next.config.js` file to include RTL-supported locales.

javascript

```
module.exports = {
  i18n: {
    locales: ["en", "es", "fr", "ar", "he"],
// Arabic and Hebrew added
    defaultLocale: "en",
  },
};
```

This enables **built-in internationalization** and ensures RTL languages are recognized.

12.2.3 Adding RTL Support in Global Styles

Modify your global CSS file (`styles/globals.css`) to support both **LTR and RTL** layouts.

css
```
html {
  direction: ltr;
  text-align: left;
}
```

```css
html[dir="rtl"] {
  direction: rtl;
  text-align: right;
}
```

This ensures that whenever the **HTML `dir` attribute** is set to `"rtl"`, the layout switches accordingly.

12.2.4 Dynamically Switching RTL and LTR

To toggle between RTL and LTR dynamically, modify `_app.js`.

javascript

```javascript
import { useRouter } from "next/router";
import { useEffect } from "react";

export default function MyApp({ Component,
pageProps }) {
  const { locale } = useRouter();

  useEffect(() => {

document.documentElement.setAttribute("dir",
locale === "ar" || locale === "he" ? "rtl" :
"ltr");
  }, [locale]);

  return <Component {...pageProps} />;
}
```

Explanation

- The `useRouter` hook fetches the current **language locale**.

- The `useEffect` hook dynamically sets the `dir` **attribute** on the `<html>` element based on the selected language.

- If the locale is `ar` (Arabic) or `he` (Hebrew), the direction switches to **RTL**.

12.2.5 Creating an RTL-Compatible Layout

For complex layouts, apply conditional **flexbox adjustments** to handle RTL variations.

Modify `styles/Layout.module.css`:

css

```css
.container {
  display: flex;
  flex-direction: row;
}

html[dir="rtl"] .container {
  flex-direction: row-reverse;
}
```

Modify `components/Layout.js` to use this styling:

javascript

```javascript
import                    styles                    from
"../styles/Layout.module.css";

export default function Layout({ children }) {
  return                                        <div
className={styles.container}>{children}</div>
;
}
```

This ensures that **navigation bars, sidebars, and UI components** are mirrored for RTL layouts.

12.2.6 Language-Specific Styles in Components

Sometimes, individual components need **RTL adjustments**. Use **CSS utility classes** to handle this.

Modify `styles/utils.css`:

css

```css
.text {
  text-align: left;
}

html[dir="rtl"] .text {
  text-align: right;
```

```
}
```

Apply this in components:

javascript

```javascript
export default function WelcomeText() {
  return <p className="text">Welcome to our
website</p>;
}
```

Now, text alignment switches automatically based on the language.

12.2.7 Using `next-intl` for Translations with RTL Support

For managing translations efficiently, use the `next-intl` library.

Step 1: Install `next-intl`
sh

```sh
npm install next-intl
```

Step 2: Define RTL Translations

Create JSON files inside a `locales` directory:

`locales/en.json`

json

```json
{
  "welcome": "Welcome to our website"
}
```

`locales/ar.json`

json

```json
{
  "welcome": "مرحبًا بك في موقعنا"
}
```

Step 3: Load Translations in Components

Modify `components/Welcome.js`:

javascript

```javascript
import { useTranslations } from "next-intl";

export default function Welcome() {
  const t = useTranslations();

  return <h1>{t("welcome")}</h1>;
}
```

Now, the welcome message updates based on the selected language.

12.2.8 Adjusting Images and Icons for RTL

Some UI elements, such as **icons and arrows**, need mirroring for RTL layouts.

Example: Mirroring icons in RTL mode using CSS

```css
.icon {
  transform: scaleX(1);
}

html[dir="rtl"] .icon {
  transform: scaleX(-1);
}
```

Now, **icons such as arrows and checkmarks** automatically flip when in RTL mode.

12.2.9 Using RTL-Compatible UI Libraries

To avoid manually adjusting every component, use **RTL-supported UI libraries** such as:

- **Material-UI** (`@mui/material`) – Supports automatic RTL adjustments.

- **Ant Design** (antd) – Has built-in RTL support.

Example: Enabling RTL in Material-UI

javascript

```javascript
import { createTheme, ThemeProvider } from
"@mui/material/styles";
import        CssBaseline        from
"@mui/material/CssBaseline";
import { useRouter } from "next/router";

export default function MyApp({ Component,
pageProps }) {
  const { locale } = useRouter();

  const theme = createTheme({
    direction: locale === "ar" || locale ===
"he" ? "rtl" : "ltr",
  });

  return (
    <ThemeProvider theme={theme}>
      <CssBaseline />
      <Component {...pageProps} />
    </ThemeProvider>
  );
}
```

Now, **Material-UI components automatically switch to RTL mode**.

12.3 Accessibility Best Practices for Next.js Apps

Ensuring **web accessibility (a11y)** is crucial for building inclusive web applications. Accessibility is not just about compliance; it enhances usability for all users, including those with disabilities. In this section, we will cover:

- The **importance of accessibility** in web applications.

- Best practices for **semantic HTML** and **ARIA attributes**.

- Implementing **keyboard navigation** and **focus management**.

- Enhancing accessibility with **Next.js features**.

- Testing accessibility using **automated tools and manual techniques**.

12.3.1 Understanding Web Accessibility

Web accessibility ensures that applications are usable by people with diverse abilities, including:

- **Visually impaired users** who rely on screen readers.

- **Users with motor disabilities** who navigate via keyboard or assistive technologies.

- **Cognitively impaired users** who need clear and consistent navigation.

Accessibility is a **legal requirement** in many regions (e.g., **WCAG, ADA, and Section 508** compliance), but it also improves **SEO and user experience** for all visitors.

12.3.2 Using Semantic HTML for Better Accessibility

Semantic HTML provides meaning to content, making it easier for **screen readers** and search engines to interpret.

Example: Incorrect vs. Correct HTML

Incorrect (Non-Semantic HTML):

html
```
<div    onclick="location.href='/about'">About
Us</div>
```

Correct (Semantic HTML with `<button>`):

html
```
<button
onclick="location.href='/about'">About
Us</button>
```

Screen readers recognize `<button>` elements as interactive, improving accessibility.

Key Semantic Elements

HTML Element	Purpose
`<header>`	Defines page headers.
`<nav>`	Marks the navigation section.
`<main>`	Identifies the main content.
`<article>`	Represents standalone content.
`<section>`	Groups related content.
`<footer>`	Contains footer information.

Using these elements improves both **screen reader navigation** and **SEO rankings**.

12.3.3 Implementing ARIA Attributes

Accessible Rich Internet Applications (ARIA) attributes enhance accessibility when standard HTML is insufficient.

Example: Using `aria-label` for Better Navigation

html

```
<button aria-label="Close menu">✖</button>
```

Example: Using `aria-live` for Dynamic Content Updates

For real-time updates, such as notifications, use `aria-live` to notify screen readers.

392

html
```
<div aria-live="polite">
  Your changes have been saved.
</div>
```

Common ARIA Attributes

Attribute	Purpose	Example
aria-label	Provides an accessible label.	`<button aria-label="Search">🔍</button>`
aria-labelledby	References another element's ID for labeling.	`<div aria-labelledby="title">`
aria-live	Announces content updates.	`<div aria-live="assertive">Error!</div>`
aria-hidden	Hides elements from screen readers.	`<div aria-hidden="true">`

Use ARIA **sparingly**, as **semantic HTML is always preferred over ARIA**.

12.3.4 Enabling Keyboard Navigation

Many users rely on **keyboard navigation** instead of a mouse. Ensure all interactive elements are keyboard-accessible.

Example: Ensuring Focus on Modal Open

javascript

```javascript
import { useRef, useEffect } from "react";

export default function Modal({ isOpen,
onClose }) {
  const modalRef = useRef(null);

  useEffect(() => {
    if (isOpen) {
      modalRef.current?.focus();
    }
  }, [isOpen]);

  return isOpen ? (
    <div     ref={modalRef}     tabIndex="-1"
role="dialog" aria-modal="true">
      <p>Modal content</p>
      <button
onClick={onClose}>Close</button>
    </div>
  ) : null;
}
```

Keyboard Navigation Checklist

- Ensure elements have a **logical tab order** using `tabindex`.

- Use `:focus` styles to highlight **active elements**.

- Avoid removing **focus outlines** unless replacing them with custom styles.

12.3.5 Enhancing Accessibility with Next.js

1. Using `next/image` for Accessible Images

The `next/image` component improves **performance and accessibility** by requiring an `alt` attribute.

javascript
```javascript
import Image from "next/image";

<Image src="/logo.png" alt="Company Logo" width={200} height={50} />;
```

2. Handling Page Titles Dynamically

Use `next/head` to set descriptive page titles and improve screen reader navigation.

javascript

```javascript
import Head from "next/head";
```

```
export default function AboutPage() {
  return (
    <>
      <Head>
        <title>About Us - MyWebsite</title>
      </Head>
      <h1>About Us</h1>
    </>
  );
}
```

3. Managing Focus on Page Transitions

Next.js offers `next/router` for handling **focus shifts on navigation**.

javascript
```javascript
import { useEffect } from "react";
import { useRouter } from "next/router";

export default function App({ Component, pageProps }) {
  const router = useRouter();

  useEffect(() => {
    const handleRouteChange = () => {
      document.getElementById("main-content")?.focus();
    };
    router.events.on("routeChangeComplete", handleRouteChange);
```

```
    return                    ()                  =>
router.events.off("routeChangeComplete",
handleRouteChange);
  }, [router]);

  return (
    <main id="main-content" tabIndex="-1">
      <Component {...pageProps} />
    </main>
  );
}
```

This ensures **screen readers and keyboard users** can immediately focus on new content after navigation.

12.3.6 Testing and Auditing Accessibility

1. Using Automated Tools

- **Lighthouse (Chrome DevTools)** – Run accessibility audits directly in DevTools.

- **axe DevTools** – Browser extension for detecting WCAG violations.

- **Wave (WebAIM)** – Web accessibility evaluation tool.

2. Manual Accessibility Testing

- **Keyboard navigation:** Use `Tab` and `Shift + Tab` to ensure logical focus flow.

- **Screen reader testing:** Use VoiceOver (macOS), NVDA (Windows), or JAWS.

- **Color contrast testing:** Verify readability with **contrast checkers** like the **WebAIM contrast checker**.

12.4 Testing for Accessibility Compliance

Ensuring web accessibility is not just about following best practices—it requires **thorough testing** to verify that applications are truly inclusive. Accessibility testing involves **automated tools, manual inspection, and user testing** to identify and resolve issues affecting users with disabilities.

In this section, we will cover:

- The importance of **accessibility testing**.

- Automated testing tools for **quick accessibility checks**.

- Manual testing techniques for **thorough validation**.

- Integrating accessibility checks into **CI/CD workflows**.

- Conducting usability tests with **real users**.

By the end of this section, you will be equipped to ensure your Next.js applications meet **Web Content Accessibility Guidelines (WCAG) 2.1 and beyond**.

12.4.1 Understanding Accessibility Compliance

Accessibility testing ensures compliance with international **standards and regulations**, such as:

- **WCAG 2.1** (Web Content Accessibility Guidelines) – The most widely accepted standard, categorized into three levels:

    ○ **A (Minimum)** – Basic web accessibility requirements.

    ○ **AA (Recommended)** – The standard for legal compliance.

    ○ **AAA (Enhanced)** – The highest level, ideal but not mandatory.

- **ADA (Americans with Disabilities Act)** – U.S. law requiring digital accessibility.

- **Section 508** – U.S. federal standard for government websites.

- **EN 301 549** – European accessibility standard.

Most applications aim for **WCAG 2.1 AA compliance** to meet industry standards.

12.4.2 Automated Accessibility Testing

Automated tools can quickly detect common accessibility issues, such as **missing alt attributes, low contrast, and improper ARIA usage**.

1. Running Accessibility Tests with Lighthouse

Lighthouse is a **built-in Chrome DevTools** tool for auditing accessibility.

Steps to Run a Lighthouse Audit

1. Open **Chrome DevTools** `(Right-click → Inspect → Go to "Lighthouse" tab)`.
2. Select **Accessibility** and run the audit.
3. Review **issues and suggestions**.

Example output:

- Contrast issues in text.
- Missing `alt` attributes on images.
- Improper ARIA roles.

2. Using axe DevTools for More Detailed Reports

axe DevTools is an advanced tool for accessibility audits.

Installation

1. Install the **axe Chrome extension**.
2. `Open DevTools → Navigate to the "axe DevTools"` tab.
3. Click **"Scan All of My Page"** to detect accessibility violations.

3. Automating Accessibility Tests in Next.js

To integrate accessibility testing into development, use **axe-core** in your test setup.

Installing `jest-axe`

bash

```
npm install --save-dev jest-axe @testing-library/react
```

Example: Writing an Accessibility Test

javascript

```
import { render } from "@testing-library/react";
import { axe, toHaveNoViolations } from "jest-axe";
import HomePage from "../pages/index";

expect.extend(toHaveNoViolations);

test("HomePage should have no accessibility violations", async () => {
  const { container } = render(<HomePage />);
  const results = await axe(container);
  expect(results).toHaveNoViolations();
});
```

Run the test:

bash

```
npm test
```

If violations exist, they will be listed in the test output.

12.4.3 Manual Accessibility Testing

Automated tools cannot detect **all accessibility issues**, such as:

- Poor **keyboard navigation**.

- Incorrect **focus order**.

- Issues with **screen readers**.

1. Keyboard Navigation Testing

Manually test navigation using only the **keyboard**:

- **Tab** – Move forward through interactive elements.

- **Shift + Tab** – Move backward.

- **Enter / Space** – Activate buttons or links.

- **Arrow keys** – Navigate dropdowns and menus.

Example: Ensuring a Modal is Focusable
javascript

```jsx
import { useEffect, useRef } from "react";

export default function Modal({ isOpen,
onClose }) {
  const modalRef = useRef(null);

  useEffect(() => {
    if (isOpen) {
      modalRef.current?.focus();
    }
  }, [isOpen]);

  return isOpen ? (
    <div      ref={modalRef}      tabIndex="-1"
role="dialog" aria-modal="true">
      <p>Modal content</p>
      <button
onClick={onClose}>Close</button>
    </div>
  ) : null;
}
```

2. Screen Reader Testing

Test with **screen readers** to verify accessibility:

- **VoiceOver (macOS)** – Built-in screen reader (Cmd + F5).

- **NVDA (Windows)** – Free screen reader (NV Access).

- **JAWS (Windows)** – Commercial screen reader (Freedom Scientific).

Verify that:

- Content is **read in the correct order**.

- Descriptive text is available for **images, buttons, and links**.

- Focus moves logically across the page.

3. Color Contrast Testing

Ensure that text has **sufficient contrast** for readability.

Use tools like:

- WebAIM Contrast Checker.

- Accessible Colors.

Contrast ratio requirements:

- **Normal text:** At least **4.5:1**.

- **Large text:** At least **3:1**.

Example of failing contrast:

css

```
button {
```

```css
  color: #888; /* Too light */
  background: #fff;
}
```

Improved contrast:

css

```css
button {
  color: #333; /* Darker text */
  background: #fff;
}
```

12.4.4 Integrating Accessibility Testing in CI/CD

Accessibility tests should be automated in **continuous integration (CI/CD) pipelines** to catch issues before deployment.

1. Adding pa11y for Command-Line Testing

Install pa11y:

bash

```bash
npm install -g pa11y
```

Run a test on a local Next.js app:

bash

```
pa11y http://localhost:3000
```

2. Running Accessibility Tests in GitHub Actions

Create a `.github/workflows/accessibility.yml` file:

yaml

```
name: Accessibility Testing
on: [push]

jobs:
  test-accessibility:
    runs-on: ubuntu-latest
    steps:
      - uses: actions/checkout@v3
      - name: Install dependencies
        run: npm install
      - name: Run accessibility tests
        run: npm run test:accessibility
```

This ensures accessibility compliance on every code push.

12.4.5 Conducting User Testing for Accessibility

The most effective way to test accessibility is to get **real users** involved.

1. Involving Users with Disabilities

Consider recruiting users who rely on:

- **Screen readers**.

- **Keyboard navigation**.

- **Assistive technologies**.

Use structured testing sessions with real-world tasks to gather **feedback on usability**.

2. Gathering Feedback

Use methods such as:

- **Surveys and interviews** with users.

- **Session recordings** to analyze behavior.

- **A/B testing** for different accessibility implementations.

Chapter 13: Building a Full-Stack Blog Application

A blog application is an excellent way to apply **full-stack Next.js development skills**. This chapter will guide you through building a **scalable and secure** blog with Next.js and MongoDB, implementing **CRUD operations**, adding **authentication for admin users**, and **deploying** the application.

What You Will Learn

- **Setting up a Next.js blog with MongoDB** for database management.
- **Building CRUD functionality** to manage blog posts dynamically.
- **Implementing authentication** to protect admin access.
- **Deploying and optimizing** the blog for production use.

By the end of this chapter, you will have a **fully functional, production-ready blog** built with Next.js 15.

13.1 Setting Up a Blog with Next.js and MongoDB

A blog application is an excellent project to learn **full-stack development with Next.js 15**. In this section, we will set up the **Next.js project**, configure a **MongoDB database**, and create a **database connection utility** to interact with MongoDB.

13.1.1 Initializing the Next.js Project

Installing Next.js 15

First, create a new Next.js application using the latest version:

bash

```
npx create-next-app@latest nextjs-blog
cd nextjs-blog
```

You will be prompted to select features. Ensure the following are enabled:

- TypeScript (optional but recommended)

- ESLint for code linting

- Tailwind CSS (optional for styling)

- App Router (default in Next.js 15)

Installing Required Dependencies

To connect our Next.js application with MongoDB, install **Mongoose** for database interactions and **dotenv** for environment variable management:

bash

```
npm install mongoose dotenv
```

13.1.2 Connecting Next.js to MongoDB

Setting Up Environment Variables

Next.js allows environment variables through a `.env.local` file. Create this file in the project root and add the MongoDB connection string:

bash

```
MONGODB_URI=mongodb+srv://your_username:your_password@cluster.mongodb.net/blog
```

Replace `your_username` and `your_password` with your actual database credentials.

Creating the Database Connection Utility

To ensure efficient database connections, we will create a **utility function** to manage MongoDB connections.

Create a new folder `lib` inside the project root and add a file `mongodb.js`:

javascript

```javascript
import mongoose from "mongoose";

const MONGODB_URI = process.env.MONGODB_URI;

if (!MONGODB_URI) {
```

```
  throw new Error("MONGODB_URI is missing in
.env.local");

}

let cached = global.mongoose || { conn: null,
promise: null };

export async function connectToDatabase() {

  if (cached.conn) return cached.conn; //
Return existing connection if available

  if (!cached.promise) {

    cached.promise                        =
mongoose.connect(MONGODB_URI, {

      useNewUrlParser: true,

      useUnifiedTopology: true,

    });

  }

  cached.conn = await cached.promise;

  return cached.conn;

}
```

Explanation

- The function **connectToDatabase** manages the database connection efficiently by caching it.

- The `cached` object prevents unnecessary reconnections, improving performance.

- If `MONGODB_URI` is missing, an error is thrown to prevent misconfiguration.

This setup ensures that our **Next.js API routes and components** can easily interact with MongoDB.

13.1.3 Defining the Blog Post Model

Now that the database connection is established, we need a **Mongoose schema** to define the structure of our blog posts.

Create a `models` folder inside the project root and add a file `Post.js`:

javascript

```javascript
import mongoose from "mongoose";

const PostSchema = new mongoose.Schema(
  {
    title: { type: String, required: true },
    content: { type: String, required: true },
```

```
    author: { type: String, required: true },

    published: { type: Boolean, default: false
},

  },

  { timestamps: true } // Automatically add
createdAt and updatedAt fields

);
```

```
export    default    mongoose.models.Post    ||
mongoose.model("Post", PostSchema);
```

Explanation

- **title, content, and author** are required fields to store blog post details.

- The **published** field determines if a post is publicly visible.

- **timestamps** automatically add createdAt and updatedAt fields to track modifications.

With this schema in place, we can now **store, retrieve, and manage blog posts** using MongoDB.

13.1.4 Verifying the Database Connection

Before proceeding, let's test our database connection by creating a simple API route.

Create a new file `pages/api/test-db.js`:

javascript

```javascript
import { connectToDatabase } from "../../lib/mongodb";

export default async function handler(req, res) {

  try {

    await connectToDatabase();

    res.status(200).json({ message: "Database connected successfully" });

  } catch (error) {

    res.status(500).json({ message: "Database connection failed", error });

  }

}
```

Running the Test

Start the Next.js development server:

bash

```
npm run dev
```

Then, open a browser and navigate to:

bash

```
http://localhost:3000/api/test-db
```

If everything is set up correctly, you should see a JSON response confirming that the **database connection was successful**.

13.2 Implementing CRUD Operations for Blog Posts

In this section, we will implement **CRUD (Create, Read, Update, Delete) operations** for our blog application using **Next.js API routes and MongoDB**. These operations will allow us to manage blog posts effectively.

13.2.1 Creating Blog Posts

To create new blog posts, we will define an **API route** that handles HTTP POST requests.

Creating the API Route

Create a new folder `pages/api/posts`, then add a file `index.js`:

```javascript
import { connectToDatabase } from
"../../../lib/mongodb";

import Post from "../../../models/Post";

export default async function handler(req,
res) {

  await connectToDatabase(); // Ensure
database connection

  if (req.method === "POST") {

    try {

      const { title, content, author } =
req.body;

      if (!title || !content || !author) {

        return res.status(400).json({
message: "All fields are required" });

      }

      const newPost = new Post({ title,
content, author });

      await newPost.save();

      return res.status(201).json({ message:
"Post created", post: newPost });

    } catch (error) {
```

```
      return  res.status(500).json({ message:
"Server error", error });

    }

  }

  res.status(405).json({ message: "Method not
allowed" });

}
```

Explanation

- The function **connectToDatabase** ensures the MongoDB connection.

- If the request method is POST, it extracts title, content, and author from the request body.

- If any field is missing, it returns a 400 Bad Request response.

- A new Post document is created and saved in MongoDB.

- On success, it returns a 201 Created response with the saved post.

Testing the API

Start the Next.js server and use **Postman** or **cURL** to send a POST request:

417

json

```
POST http://localhost:3000/api/posts

Content-Type: application/json

{

  "title": "My First Blog Post",

  "content": "This is the content of the blog
post.",

  "author": "John Doe"

}
```

A successful response should include the saved post details.

13.2.2 Retrieving Blog Posts

Next, we will implement **fetching all blog posts** and **retrieving a single blog post by ID**.

Fetching All Posts

Modify the existing `pages/api/posts/index.js` to handle `GET` requests:

javascript

```javascript
export default async function handler(req,
res) {

  await connectToDatabase();

  if (req.method === "GET") {

    try {

      const posts = await Post.find().sort({
createdAt: -1 }); // Fetch all posts, newest
first

      return res.status(200).json(posts);

    } catch (error) {

      return res.status(500).json({ message:
"Server error", error });

    }

  }


  if (req.method === "POST") {

    try {

      const { title, content, author } =
req.body;
```

```javascript
    if (!title || !content || !author) {

        return          res.status(400).json({
message: "All fields are required" });

    }

    const newPost = new Post({ title,
content, author });

    await newPost.save();

    return res.status(201).json({ message:
"Post created", post: newPost });

  } catch (error) {

    return res.status(500).json({ message:
"Server error", error });

    }

  }

  res.status(405).json({ message: "Method not
allowed" });

}
```

Fetching a Single Post

Create a new API route pages/api/posts/[id].js:

javascript

```javascript
import { connectToDatabase } from
"../../../lib/mongodb";
```

420

```javascript
import Post from "../../../models/Post";

export default async function handler(req,
res) {

  await connectToDatabase();

  const { id } = req.query; // Extract post ID
from request URL

  if (req.method === "GET") {

    try {

      const post = await Post.findById(id);

      if (!post) {

        return          res.status(404).json({
message: "Post not found" });

      }

      return res.status(200).json(post);

    } catch (error) {

      return  res.status(500).json({  message:
"Server error", error });

    }

  }
```

```
    res.status(405).json({ message: "Method not
allowed" });

}
```

Testing

To retrieve all posts:

http

```
GET http://localhost:3000/api/posts
```

To retrieve a single post by ID:

http

```
GET http://localhost:3000/api/posts/<POST_ID>
```

13.2.3 Updating Blog Posts

To update a post, we will handle PUT requests in
pages/api/posts/[id].js:

javascript

```
export default async function handler(req,
res) {

  await connectToDatabase();

  const { id } = req.query;
```

```javascript
if (req.method === "PUT") {

  try {

    const { title, content, author,
published } = req.body;

    const updatedPost = await
Post.findByIdAndUpdate(

      id,

      { title, content, author, published },

      { new: true, runValidators: true }

    );

    if (!updatedPost) {

      return res.status(404).json({
message: "Post not found" });

    }

    return res.status(200).json({ message:
"Post updated", post: updatedPost });

  } catch (error) {

    return res.status(500).json({ message:
"Server error", error });

  }

}
```

```
    res.status(405).json({ message: "Method not
allowed" });
```

}

Testing

Send a PUT request with updated data:

json

```
PUT http://localhost:3000/api/posts/<POST_ID>

Content-Type: application/json


{

  "title": "Updated Blog Post",

  "content": "Updated content here.",

  "author": "John Doe",

  "published": true

}
```

A successful response will return the updated post.

13.2.4 Deleting Blog Posts

Finally, we will handle DELETE requests in pages/api/posts/[id].js:

javascript

```javascript
export default async function handler(req,
res) {

  await connectToDatabase();

  const { id } = req.query;


  if (req.method === "DELETE") {

    try {

      const deletedPost = await
Post.findByIdAndDelete(id);

      if (!deletedPost) {

        return res.status(404).json({
message: "Post not found" });

      }


      return res.status(200).json({ message:
"Post deleted" });
```

```
    } catch (error) {

      return  res.status(500).json({  message:
"Server error", error });

    }

  }

  res.status(405).json({ message: "Method not
allowed" });

}
```

Testing

To delete a post:

http

```
DELETE
http://localhost:3000/api/posts/<POST_ID>
```

A successful response will confirm the deletion.

13.3 Adding Authentication for Blog Admins

To secure our blog administration panel, we need to implement
authentication and authorization. In this section, we will set up
authentication using **NextAuth.js**, a widely used authentication library
for Next.js. We will also ensure that only authenticated users with **admin
privileges** can create, update, or delete blog posts.

13.3.1 Installing NextAuth.js and Configuring Authentication

Step 1: Install Dependencies

Run the following command to install **NextAuth.js** and **bcrypt** for password hashing:

sh

```
npm install next-auth bcrypt mongoose
```

Step 2: Setting Up Authentication

Create a new folder `pages/api/auth`, then add a file `[...nextauth].js`:

javascript

```
import NextAuth from "next-auth";

import CredentialsProvider from "next-auth/providers/credentials";

import { connectToDatabase } from "../../../lib/mongodb";

import User from "../../../models/User";

import bcrypt from "bcrypt";


export default NextAuth({

  providers: [
```

```
CredentialsProvider({

    name: "Credentials",

    credentials: {

        email: { label: "Email", type:
"email", placeholder: "admin@example.com" },

        password: { label: "Password", type:
"password" },

    },

    async authorize(credentials) {

        await connectToDatabase();


        const user = await User.findOne({
email: credentials.email });

        if (!user) {

            throw new Error("No user found with
this email.");

        }


        const isValid = await
bcrypt.compare(credentials.password,
user.password);

        if (!isValid) {
```

```javascript
        throw        new        Error("Invalid
password.");

        }

        return  {   id:   user._id,   name:
user.name, email: user.email, role: user.role
};

    },

  }),

 ],

 callbacks: {

   async session({ session, token }) {

     session.user = token.user;

     return session;

   },

   async jwt({ token, user }) {

     if (user) {

       token.user = user;

     }

     return token;

   },

 },
```

```
    secret: process.env.NEXTAUTH_SECRET,

    session: { strategy: "jwt" },

});
```

Explanation

- Uses **NextAuth.js** with `CredentialsProvider` for email/password login.

- Connects to the database and verifies the user's credentials.

- Uses **bcrypt** to securely compare passwords.

- Returns **JWT-based sessions** with user details, including the role.

13.3.2 Creating an Admin User

Before logging in, we need an **admin user** in the database.

Step 1: Define a User Model

Create `models/User.js`:

javascript

```
import mongoose from "mongoose";

const UserSchema = new mongoose.Schema({
```

```javascript
  name: String,

  email: { type: String, unique: true },

  password: String,

  role: { type: String, enum: ["admin",
"editor", "user"], default: "user" },

});

export default mongoose.models.User ||
mongoose.model("User", UserSchema);
```

Step 2: Create an Admin User in MongoDB

Run this script to create an **admin user**:

javascript

```javascript
import mongoose from "mongoose";

import bcrypt from "bcrypt";

import User from "../models/User";

import dotenv from "dotenv";

dotenv.config();

mongoose.connect(process.env.MONGODB_URI);

async function createAdminUser() {
```

```javascript
  const existingAdmin = await User.findOne({
email: "admin@example.com" });

  if (existingAdmin) {

    console.log("Admin user already exists.");

    return;

  }

  const        hashedPassword        =        await
bcrypt.hash("admin123", 10);

  const admin = new User({

    name: "Admin User",

    email: "admin@example.com",

    password: hashedPassword,

    role: "admin",

  });

  await admin.save();

  console.log("Admin user created.");

  mongoose.connection.close();

}

createAdminUser();
```

Run the script using:

sh

```
node scripts/createAdminUser.js
```

This will create an **admin user** with the following credentials:

- **Email:** admin@example.com

- **Password:** admin123

13.3.3 Protecting API Routes

Now, we need to **restrict access** to API routes that modify blog posts.

Step 1: Create a Middleware to Check Authentication

Create middleware/auth.js:

javascript

```
import { getSession } from "next-auth/react";

export async function authenticate(req, res,
next) {

  const session = await getSession({ req });

  if (!session || session.user.role !==
"admin") {

    return res.status(403).json({ message:
"Unauthorized" });
```

```
  }

  next();

}
```

Step 2: Apply Authentication to API Routes

Modify `pages/api/posts/index.js` to restrict post creation:

javascript

```
import { authenticate } from
"../../../middleware/auth";

export default async function handler(req,
res) {

  await connectToDatabase();

  if (req.method === "POST") {

    await authenticate(req, res, async () => {

      const { title, content, author } =
req.body;

      if (!title || !content || !author) {

        return        res.status(400).json({
message: "All fields are required" });

      }
```

```javascript
    const newPost = new Post({ title,
content, author });

    await newPost.save();

    return res.status(201).json({ message:
"Post created", post: newPost });

    });

  }

  if (req.method === "GET") {

    const posts = await Post.find();

    return res.status(200).json(posts);

  }

  res.status(405).json({ message: "Method not
allowed" });

}
```

Similarly, update `pages/api/posts/[id].js` to protect update and delete actions:

javascript

```javascript
import { authenticate } from
"../../../middleware/auth";

export default async function handler(req,
res) {

  await connectToDatabase();
```

435

```javascript
const { id } = req.query;

if (req.method === "PUT") {

  await authenticate(req, res, async () => {

    const { title, content } = req.body;

    const updatedPost = await
Post.findByIdAndUpdate(id, { title, content },
{ new: true });

    if (!updatedPost) {

      return res.status(404).json({
message: "Post not found" });

    }

    return res.status(200).json({ message:
"Post updated", post: updatedPost });

  });

}

if (req.method === "DELETE") {

  await authenticate(req, res, async () => {

    const deletedPost = await
Post.findByIdAndDelete(id);

    if (!deletedPost) {

      return res.status(404).json({
message: "Post not found" });
```

```
    }

    return res.status(200).json({ message:
"Post deleted" });

  });

  }

  res.status(405).json({ message: "Method not
allowed" });

}
```

13.3.4 Implementing   Admin   Dashboard Authentication

Now, we will create a **protected admin dashboard**.

Step 1: Add Authentication to the Admin Page

Create pages/admin.js:

javascript

```
import { getSession } from "next-auth/react";

import { useRouter } from "next/router";

import { useEffect, useState } from "react";

export default function Admin() {
```

```
  const       [loading,       setLoading]      =
useState(true);

  const       [session,       setSession]      =
useState(null);

  const router = useRouter();

  useEffect(() => {

    getSession().then((session) => {

      if (!session || session.user.role !==
"admin") {

        router.replace("/login");

      } else {

        setSession(session);

      }

      setLoading(false);

    });

  }, []);


  if (loading) return <p>Loading...</p>;

  if (!session) return null;

  return (

    <div>
```

```
<h1>Admin Dashboard</h1>

<p>Welcome, {session.user.name}</p>

<button            onClick={()            =>
signOut()}>Logout</button>

  </div>

 );

}
```

13.4 Deploying and Optimizing the Blog

After implementing authentication and finalizing the core functionality of our blog, the next step is to deploy it to a live environment and optimize its performance. This chapter will guide you through deploying your Next.js blog and applying key optimizations to improve speed, SEO, and scalability.

13.4.1 Choosing a Deployment Platform

Next.js applications can be deployed on various platforms, including Vercel, Netlify, AWS, and DigitalOcean. The best choice depends on your requirements:

- **Vercel**: Best for seamless Next.js deployments with built-in serverless functions and automatic scaling.

- **Netlify**: Ideal for static site generation (SSG) with automatic deployments from Git.

- **AWS (EC2, Amplify, Lambda)**: Suitable for custom deployments requiring more control.

- **DigitalOcean (App Platform, Droplets, Kubernetes)**: Good for developers looking for a balance of simplicity and control.

For this tutorial, we will use **Vercel**, the official deployment platform for Next.js, due to its ease of use.

13.4.2 Deploying to Vercel

Step 1: Install the Vercel CLI

Ensure you have the Vercel CLI installed:

bash

```
npm install -g vercel
```

Log in to Vercel:

bash

```
vercel login
```

Step 2: Initialize the Deployment

Navigate to your project folder and run:

bash

```
vercel
```

You will be prompted to provide configuration details. Accept the default settings unless you need custom options.

Step 3: Set Up Environment Variables

If your project requires environment variables (e.g., database connection strings, API keys), set them in Vercel:

bash

```
vercel      env      add      DATABASE_URL
"your_database_url_here"
```

Alternatively, you can add them manually in the Vercel dashboard under **Project Settings > Environment Variables**.

Step 4: Deploy the Application

Run:

bash

```
vercel --prod
```

This deploys the application to a live URL. You will receive a URL where your blog is hosted.

13.4.3 Optimizing Performance

Performance is crucial for user experience and SEO. Below are key optimizations:

Image Optimization

Use Next.js's built-in <Image> component to optimize images:

jsx

```
import Image from 'next/image';

export default function BlogImage() {

  return (

    <Image

      src="/images/blog-thumbnail.jpg"

      alt="Blog Thumbnail"

      width={800}

      height={500}

      priority

    />

  );
```

```
}
```

Lazy Loading and Code Splitting

Next.js automatically performs **code splitting**, but you can optimize it further using **dynamic imports**:

jsx

```jsx
import dynamic from 'next/dynamic';

const DynamicComponent = dynamic(() =>
import('../components/HeavyComponent'), {

  ssr: false,

  loading: () => <p>Loading...</p>,

});



export default function Page() {

  return <DynamicComponent />;

}
```

Caching and Compression

- Enable **server-side caching** using headers in
  `next.config.js`:

```js
module.exports = {
  async headers() {
    return [
      {
        source: '/(.*)',
        headers: [
          { key: 'Cache-Control', value:
'public, max-age=31536000, immutable' },
        ],
      },
    ];
  },
};
```

- Use **Gzip or Brotli compression** to reduce payload size.

13.4.4 Enhancing SEO

SEO is essential for blog visibility. Next.js provides **built-in SEO optimizations** with the <Head> component:

jsx

```
import Head from 'next/head';

export default function BlogPost({ title,
description }) {

  return (

    <>

      <Head>

        <title>{title}</title>

        <meta                    name="description"
content={description} />

        <meta  name="robots"  content="index,
follow" />

      </Head>

      <h1>{title}</h1>

      <p>{description}</p>

    </>

  );

}
```

445

Other key SEO optimizations:

- Use **canonical URLs** to prevent duplicate content issues.

- Implement **structured data (JSON-LD)** for better indexing.

13.4.5 Monitoring and Logging

Performance Monitoring

Vercel provides built-in analytics, but you can also use Google Analytics or Vercel's Edge Functions to track performance:

jsx

```
import Script from 'next/script';

export default function Analytics() {

  return (

    <Script

      strategy="afterInteractive"

src="https://www.googletagmanager.com/gtag/js?id=YOUR_TRACKING_ID"

    />
```

```
  );

}
```

Error Logging

Use **Sentry** for real-time error tracking:

bash

```
npm install @sentry/nextjs
```

Configure it in _app.js:

jsx

```
import * as Sentry from '@sentry/nextjs';

Sentry.init({

  dsn: 'YOUR_SENTRY_DSN',

  tracesSampleRate: 1.0,

});
```

13.4.6 Implementing CI/CD for Automated Deployments

For continuous integration and deployment (CI/CD), use GitHub Actions:

Step 1: Create `.github/workflows/deploy.yml`

yaml

```
name: Deploy to Vercel

on:

  push:

    branches:

      - main


jobs:

  deploy:

    runs-on: ubuntu-latest

    steps:

      - uses: actions/checkout@v3

      - name: Install dependencies

        run: npm install

      - name: Build the project

        run: npm run build

      - name: Deploy to Vercel

        run:   vercel   --prod   --token=${{
secrets.VERCEL_TOKEN }}
```

Step 2: Add Vercel Token to GitHub Secrets

1. Go to your GitHub repository.

2. Navigate to **Settings** > **Secrets** > **Actions**.

3. Add a new secret named `VERCEL_TOKEN`.

4. Paste your **Vercel token** from the Vercel dashboard.

Once set up, every push to the `main` branch will automatically trigger a deployment.

Chapter 14: Building an E-Commerce Application

E-commerce applications are among the most popular web applications today, requiring a combination of front-end and back-end technologies for product management, order processing, and secure payment handling. In this chapter, we will build a **full-stack e-commerce application** using **Next.js 15** and **Stripe** for payment processing. The application will support product listings, a shopping cart, and a checkout system.

14.1 Creating an Online Store with Next.js and Stripe

E-commerce applications require seamless integration between the front-end and back-end, with a focus on performance, security, and user experience. In this section, we will set up a **Next.js 15** project and integrate **Stripe** for payment processing. This setup will serve as the foundation for building an online store with product listings, a shopping cart, and checkout functionality.

Setting Up the Next.js Project

Before we start coding, ensure you have **Node.js 18+** installed. If not, download it from the official Node.js website.

Now, create a new Next.js application using the following command:

bash

```
npx create-next-app@latest nextjs-store
```

Navigate into the project directory:

bash

```
cd nextjs-store
```

Next, install the required dependencies for this project:

bash

```
npm install stripe next-auth @stripe/react-
stripe-js @stripe/stripe-js
```

Here is a breakdown of the dependencies:

- **stripe**: The official Stripe SDK for interacting with the Stripe API.

- **next-auth**: A library for handling authentication (if needed).

- **@stripe/react-stripe-js** and **@stripe/stripe-js**: Libraries for integrating Stripe's payment UI.

Configuring Stripe

1. Obtain API Keys

To integrate Stripe, you need API keys from the **Stripe Dashboard**.

1. Create an account on Stripe.

2. Navigate to **Developers > API Keys** in the Stripe dashboard.

3. Copy both the **Publishable Key** and **Secret Key**.

2. Store API Keys Securely

In the Next.js project, create an **environment file** `.env.local` to store the keys:

env

```
NEXT_PUBLIC_STRIPE_PUBLISHABLE_KEY=your_publi
shable_key

STRIPE_SECRET_KEY=your_secret_key
```

3. Create a Stripe Helper Function

To streamline API interactions, create a helper function in `lib/stripe.js`:

javascript

```
import Stripe from 'stripe';

// Initialize Stripe with the secret key

const stripe = new Stripe(process.env.STRIPE_SECRET_KEY, {

  apiVersion: '2024-03-12',
```

```
});

export default stripe;
```

This setup ensures that Stripe API requests are handled securely in the back end.

Setting Up a Product Catalog

A product catalog is essential for an online store. Instead of fetching products from a database for now, we will create a simple product list in `data/products.js`:

javascript

```
export const products = [

  {

    id: 1,

    name: "Wireless Headphones",

    price: 9999, // Price in cents (e.g., 9999
= $99.99)

    image: "/headphones.jpg",

    description:    "High-quality    wireless
headphones with noise cancellation.",

  },
```

```
  {
    id: 2,
    name: "Smart Watch",
    price: 14999,
    image: "/watch.jpg",
    description: "A sleek smartwatch with
multiple health tracking features.",
  }
];
```

Displaying Products on the Homepage

Now, create a **product listing page** in pages/index.js to display products dynamically:

javascript

```
import Link from 'next/link';
import { products } from '../data/products';
export default function Home() {
  return (
    <div>
      <h1>Online Store</h1>
```

```jsx
    <div style={{ display: 'flex', gap:
'20px' }}>

      {products.map((product) => (

        <div key={product.id} style={{
border: '1px solid #ddd', padding: '10px' }}>

          <img src={product.image}
alt={product.name} width="150" />

          <h2>{product.name}</h2>

          <p>Price: ${(product.price /
100).toFixed(2)}</p>

          <Link
href={`/products/${product.id}`}>

            <button>View Details</button>

          </Link>

        </div>

      ))}

    </div>

  </div>

  );

}
```

This component:

- Loops through the `products` array.

- Displays the product **image, name, price, and a button** to view details.

Creating a Product Details Page

Next.js provides **dynamic routes** to handle individual product pages.

Create a new directory `pages/products/` and add a file `[id].js`:

javascript

```javascript
import { products } from '../../data/products';

export async function getStaticPaths() {
  const paths = products.map((product) => ({
    params: { id: product.id.toString() },
  }));
  return { paths, fallback: false };
}

export async function getStaticProps({ params }) {
```

```
  const    product    =    products.find((p)    =>
p.id.toString() === params.id);

  return { props: { product } };

}

export default function ProductPage({ product
}) {

  return (

    <div>

      <h1>{product.name}</h1>

      <img                      src={product.image}
alt={product.name} width="300" />

      <p>{product.description}</p>

      <p>Price:          ${(product.price        /
100).toFixed(2)}</p>

    </div>

  );

}
```

This page:

- Uses **getStaticPaths** to generate dynamic product routes.

- Fetches product details via **getStaticProps**.

- Displays product details dynamically.

14.2 Managing Products and Orders

In an e-commerce application, managing products and orders efficiently is essential for a smooth shopping experience. This section will focus on:

- Implementing **product management** with CRUD (Create, Read, Update, Delete) operations.

- Creating an **admin dashboard** for managing inventory.

- Handling **customer orders** and integrating a backend API for order processing.

By the end of this section, you will have a fully functional system for managing products and tracking orders using **Next.js 15** and **MongoDB** (or any database of your choice).

Setting Up a MongoDB Database

For storing products and orders, we will use **MongoDB**, a NoSQL database. You can set up a **MongoDB Atlas** account or run a local instance.

1. **Sign up for MongoDB Atlas** at mongodb.com and create a free cluster.

2. **Create a database** called `nextjs_store` and a collection named `products`.

458

3. **Get the connection string** from **Database Access** > **Connect** > **Drivers** and store it in .env.local:

env

```
MONGODB_URI=mongodb+srv://your_username:your_
password@your_cluster.mongodb.net/nextjs_stor
e
```

4. Install **Mongoose** to interact with MongoDB:

bash

```
npm install mongoose
```

Connecting to MongoDB

Create a database connection file in lib/db.js:

javascript

```
import mongoose from 'mongoose';

const MONGODB_URI = process.env.MONGODB_URI;

if (!MONGODB_URI) {

  throw new Error("Please define the
MONGODB_URI environment variable.");

}
```

```
let cached = global.mongoose || { conn: null,
promise: null };

export async function connectToDatabase() {

  if (cached.conn) {

    return cached.conn;

  }

  if (!cached.promise) {

    cached.promise                           =
mongoose.connect(MONGODB_URI, {

      useNewUrlParser: true,

      useUnifiedTopology: true,

    }).then((mongoose) => mongoose);

  }


  cached.conn = await cached.promise;

  return cached.conn;

}
```

This function ensures a **single database connection** for performance optimization.

Creating a Product Model

Define the structure of a **Product** using Mongoose. Create `models/Product.js`:

javascript

```javascript
import mongoose from 'mongoose';

const ProductSchema = new mongoose.Schema({

  name: { type: String, required: true },

  price: { type: Number, required: true },

  description: { type: String, required: true
},

  image: { type: String, required: true },

  stock: { type: Number, required: true,
default: 0 },

}, { timestamps: true });


export default mongoose.models.Product ||
mongoose.model('Product', ProductSchema);
```

Each product has a **name, price, description, image, and stock count**. The timestamps help track creation and updates.

Creating API Routes for Product Management

To manage products, create the Next.js API routes under `pages/api/products.js`.

1. Fetching All Products

javascript

```javascript
import { connectToDatabase } from '../../lib/db';

import Product from '../../models/Product';

export default async function handler(req, res) {

  await connectToDatabase();

  if (req.method === 'GET') {

    const products = await Product.find({});

    return res.status(200).json(products);

  }


  return res.status(405).json({ message: 'Method Not Allowed' });

}
```

2. Adding a New Product

Modify `pages/api/products.js` to handle POST requests:

javascript

```
if (req.method === 'POST') {

  try {

    const { name, price, description, image,
stock } = req.body;

    const product = new Product({ name, price,
description, image, stock });

    await product.save();

    return res.status(201).json(product);

  } catch (error) {

    return   res.status(500).json({   message:
'Error adding product', error });

  }

}
```

3. Updating and Deleting a Product

For updates and deletion, create a **dynamic API route** in `pages/api/products/[id].js`:

javascript

```javascript
import { connectToDatabase } from
'../../../lib/db';

import Product from '../../../models/Product';

export default async function handler(req,
res) {

  await connectToDatabase();

  const { id } = req.query;

  if (req.method === 'PUT') {

    const { name, price, description, image,
stock } = req.body;

    const product = await
Product.findByIdAndUpdate(id, { name, price,
description, image, stock }, { new: true });

    return res.status(200).json(product);

  }


  if (req.method === 'DELETE') {

    await Product.findByIdAndDelete(id);

    return res.status(200).json({ message:
'Product deleted successfully' });

  }
```

```javascript
    return    res.status(405).json({    message:
'Method Not Allowed' });

}
```

Creating an Admin Dashboard

To manage products, create an admin page at pages/admin.js:

javascript

```javascript
import { useState, useEffect } from 'react';

export default function AdminPage() {

  const    [products,    setProducts]    =
useState([]);

  const    [newProduct,    setNewProduct]    =
useState({ name: '', price: '', description:
'', image: '', stock: '' });

  useEffect(() => {

    fetch('/api/products')

      .then((res) => res.json())

      .then((data) => setProducts(data));

  }, []);
```

465

```
const handleAddProduct = async () => {

  await fetch('/api/products', {

    method: 'POST',

    headers:          {          'Content-Type':
'application/json' },

    body: JSON.stringify(newProduct),

  });

  window.location.reload();

};

return (

  <div>

    <h1>Admin Dashboard</h1>

    <h2>Add Product</h2>

    <input   type="text"   placeholder="Name"
onChange={(e)        =>        setNewProduct({
...newProduct, name: e.target.value })} />

    <input                      type="number"
placeholder="Price"      onChange={(e)      =>
setNewProduct({      ...newProduct,      price:
e.target.value })} />
```

```jsx
      <input  type="text"  placeholder="Image
URL"   onChange={(e)   =>   setNewProduct({
...newProduct, image: e.target.value })} />

      <input                       type="number"
placeholder="Stock"        onChange={(e)        =>
setNewProduct({      ...newProduct,      stock:
e.target.value })} />

      <button  onClick={handleAddProduct}>Add
Product</button>

      <h2>Existing Products</h2>

      <ul>

        {products.map((product) => (

          <li key={product._id}>

            {product.name} - ${(product.price
/ 100).toFixed(2)}

          </li>

        ))}

      </ul>

    </div>

  );
}
```

This admin page:

- Fetches all products.
- Provides a form for adding new products.
- Displays existing products.

Managing Orders

Creating an Order Model

Define `models/Order.js`:

javascript

```javascript
import mongoose from 'mongoose';

const OrderSchema = new mongoose.Schema({

  user: { type: String, required: true },

  products: [{ productId: String, quantity: Number }],

  total: { type: Number, required: true },

  status: { type: String, default: 'Pending' },

}, { timestamps: true });

export default mongoose.models.Order || mongoose.model('Order', OrderSchema);
```

Handling Orders in the API

Create `pages/api/orders.js` to process orders:

javascript

```javascript
import { connectToDatabase } from '../../lib/db';

import Order from '../../models/Order';

export default async function handler(req, res) {
  await connectToDatabase();

  if (req.method === 'POST') {

    const { user, products, total } = req.body;

    const order = new Order({ user, products, total });

    await order.save();

    return res.status(201).json(order);

  }

  if (req.method === 'GET') {

    const orders = await Order.find({});

    return res.status(200).json(orders);

  }
```

```
    return    res.status(405).json({    message:
'Method Not Allowed' });

}
```

14.3 Implementing Secure Payment Processing

In this section, we will implement secure payment processing in our Next.js 15 e-commerce application using **Stripe**. Stripe is a widely used payment gateway that provides a robust and developer-friendly API for handling transactions securely.

This section will cover:

1. **Setting up Stripe in a Next.js project**
2. **Creating a checkout session for payments**
3. **Handling payment success and failures**
4. **Securing payment processing using webhooks**

By the end of this section, users will be able to complete transactions securely within the e-commerce application.

14.3.1 Setting Up Stripe

Step 1: Creating a Stripe Account

1. Sign up at Stripe and create an account.

2. Navigate to **Developers > API Keys** and retrieve the **Publishable Key** and **Secret Key**.

3. Store these in your `.env.local` file:

env

```
STRIPE_PUBLIC_KEY=your_publishable_key

STRIPE_SECRET_KEY=your_secret_key
```

Step 2: Installing Stripe SDK

Install Stripe's Node.js SDK in your Next.js project:

bash

```
npm install stripe
```

14.3.2 Creating a Checkout Session

Stripe's checkout session will handle the payment process. Create an API route in `pages/api/checkout.js`:

javascript

```
import Stripe from 'stripe';

const         stripe         =         new
Stripe(process.env.STRIPE_SECRET_KEY);

export  default  async  function  handler(req,
res) {

  if (req.method !== 'POST') {
```

```
    return   res.status(405).json({  message:
'Method Not Allowed' });

  }


  try {

    const { products } = req.body;

    const lineItems = products.map((product)
=> ({

      price_data: {

        currency: 'usd',

        product_data: {

          name: product.name,

        },

        unit_amount: product.price * 100,

      },

      quantity: product.quantity,

    }));

    const       session       =       await
stripe.checkout.sessions.create({

      payment_method_types: ['card'],

      line_items: lineItems,
```

```
    mode: 'payment',

    success_url:
`${req.headers.origin}/success?session_id={CH
ECKOUT_SESSION_ID}`,

    cancel_url:
`${req.headers.origin}/cancel`,

  });

  res.status(200).json({        sessionId:
session.id });

} catch (error) {

  res.status(500).json({  message:   'Error
creating    checkout    session',    error:
error.message });

  }

}
```

Explanation:

- `line_items`: Converts product data into a Stripe-compatible format.

- `checkout.sessions.create`: Generates a checkout session.

- `success_url` **and** `cancel_url`: Redirect users based on transaction status.

14.3.3 Handling Checkout on the Frontend

To allow users to proceed with payment, create a CheckoutButton.js component:

javascript

```javascript
import { loadStripe } from '@stripe/stripe-js';

const stripePromise = loadStripe(process.env.NEXT_PUBLIC_STRIPE_PUBLIC_KEY);

export default function CheckoutButton({ cart }) {

  const handleCheckout = async () => {

    const stripe = await stripePromise;

    const response = await fetch('/api/checkout', {

      method: 'POST',

      headers: { 'Content-Type': 'application/json' },

      body: JSON.stringify({ products: cart }),

    });
```

```
    const    {    sessionId   }   =    await
response.json();

    await         stripe.redirectToCheckout({
sessionId });

  };

  return                            <button
onClick={handleCheckout}>Proceed            to
Payment</button>;

}
```

Explanation:

- Loads Stripe's client library.
- Sends the cart data to the checkout API.
- Redirects users to Stripe's hosted checkout page.

14.3.4 Handling Payment Success and Failures

Success Page

Create `pages/success.js`:

javascript

```
import { useRouter } from 'next/router';

export default function SuccessPage() {
```

```javascript
  const router = useRouter();

  const { session_id } = router.query;


  return (

    <div>

      <h1>Payment Successful</h1>

      <p>Thank  you  for  your  purchase.  Your
order is confirmed.</p>

      <p>Session ID: {session_id}</p>

    </div>

  );

}
```

Cancel Page

Create pages/cancel.js:

javascript

```javascript
export default function CancelPage() {

  return (

    <div>

      <h1>Payment Canceled</h1>
```

```
    <p>Your  payment  was  not  completed.
Please try again.</p>

    </div>

  );

}
```

14.3.5 Securing Payments with Webhooks

Webhooks allow Stripe to notify your application when a payment is
completed.

Step 1: Create a Webhook API

Create `pages/api/webhooks.js`:

javascript

```
import { buffer } from 'micro';

import Stripe from 'stripe';

const          stripe          =          new
Stripe(process.env.STRIPE_SECRET_KEY);

export const config = {

  api: {

    bodyParser: false,

  },
```

```javascript
};

export default async function handler(req,
res) {

  const sig = req.headers['stripe-signature'];

  const             endpointSecret             =
process.env.STRIPE_WEBHOOK_SECRET;

  let event;

  try {

    const buf = await buffer(req);

    event                                     =
stripe.webhooks.constructEvent(buf,       sig,
endpointSecret);

  } catch (err) {

    return     res.status(400).json({     error:
`Webhook Error: ${err.message}` });

  }

  if                (event.type               ===
'checkout.session.completed') {

    const session = event.data.object;

    console.log('Payment           successful:',
session);

  }
```

```
    res.status(200).json({ received: true });
}
```

Step 2: Configure the Webhook on Stripe

1. Go to **Developers** > **Webhooks** in the Stripe dashboard.

2. Click **Add Endpoint** and enter your API URL (e.g.,
    `https://yourdomain.com/api/webhooks`).

3. Select `checkout.session.completed` as the event.

4. Copy the **Signing Secret** and add it to `.env.local`:

env

```
STRIPE_WEBHOOK_SECRET=your_webhook_secret
```

14.3.6 Testing Payments Locally

To test Stripe webhooks locally, install the Stripe CLI:

bash

```
npm install -g stripe
```

Then, forward webhook events to your local server:

bash

```
stripe          listen           --forward-to
localhost:3000/api/webhooks
```

14.4 Deploying the E-Commerce App

Deploying a Next.js 15 application requires careful consideration of performance, security, and scalability. This section will guide you through deploying your e-commerce app using **Vercel**, **Docker**, and **custom cloud deployments (AWS, DigitalOcean, or Google Cloud)**.

Topics Covered:

1. **Deploying to Vercel** (Recommended for most Next.js projects)

2. **Deploying with Docker** (For containerized environments)

3. **Deploying to AWS (EC2 + Nginx + PM2)** (For full control over hosting)

4. **Deploying to DigitalOcean using App Platform**

14.4.1 Deploying to Vercel

Step 1: Install Vercel CLI

Vercel is the **official deployment platform for Next.js** and offers an optimized, serverless experience.

Install Vercel globally:

bash

```
npm install -g vercel
```

Step 2: Deploy the Application

Run the following command from your project root:

bash

```
vercel
```

You will be prompted to:

- Authenticate with your Vercel account.

- Choose a project name.

- Configure settings.

Once completed, Vercel will generate a public URL for your application.

Step 3: Set Environment Variables

Go to the **Vercel Dashboard** > **Project Settings** > **Environment Variables** and add:

plaintext

```
STRIPE_PUBLIC_KEY=your_publishable_key

STRIPE_SECRET_KEY=your_secret_key

DATABASE_URL=your_database_connection_string

NEXT_PUBLIC_API_URL=https://yourapi.com
```

Step 4: Connect a Custom Domain

1. Go to **Vercel Dashboard** > **Domains**.

2. Add your custom domain and configure the DNS settings.

Your Next.js app is now live on Vercel.

14.4.2 Deploying with Docker

If you need a **containerized deployment**, Docker provides a way to run your Next.js application in isolated environments.

Step 1: Create a Dockerfile

In your project root, create a `Dockerfile`:

dockerfile

```
# Use official Next.js image

FROM node:18-alpine

WORKDIR /app

# Copy package.json and install dependencies

COPY package.json package-lock.json ./

RUN npm install --production

# Copy the entire project

COPY . .

# Build the project

RUN npm run build

# Expose port 3000

EXPOSE 3000

# Start Next.js server

CMD ["npm", "start"]
```

Step 2: Build and Run the Docker Container

Build the image:

bash

```
docker build -t nextjs-ecommerce .
```

Run the container:

bash

```
docker run -p 3000:3000 nextjs-ecommerce
```

Your app will now be available at `http://localhost:3000`.

14.4.3 Deploying to AWS (EC2 + Nginx + PM2)

If you need full control over your hosting environment, deploying to **AWS EC2** with **Nginx and PM2** is a great option.

Step 1: Launch an EC2 Instance

1. Log in to the **AWS Management Console**.

2. Go to **EC2 > Launch Instance**.

3. Choose **Ubuntu 22.04** as the base OS.

4. Select an instance type (`t2.micro` for small applications).

5. Configure **security groups**: Allow HTTP (80), HTTPS (443), and SSH (22).

Step 2: Install Node.js and PM2

Connect to the EC2 instance using SSH:

bash

```
ssh -i your-key.pem ubuntu@your-ec2-ip
```

Install Node.js:

bash

```
curl                             -fsSL
https://deb.nodesource.com/setup_18.x | sudo -
E bash -

sudo apt install -y nodejs
```

Install PM2 (process manager for running Next.js):

bash

```
npm install -g pm2
```

Step 3: Deploy the App

1. Clone your project repository:

bash

```
git                               clone
https://github.com/yourusername/your-repo.git
```

```
cd your-repo
```

2. Install dependencies and build the project:

bash

```
npm install
npm run build
```

3. Start the Next.js app using PM2:

bash

```
pm2 start npm --name "nextjs-app" -- start
pm2 save
```

Step 4: Configure Nginx as a Reverse Proxy

1. Install Nginx:

bash

```
sudo apt install nginx -y
```

2. Edit the Nginx configuration file:

bash

```bash
sudo nano /etc/nginx/sites-available/default
```

Replace the contents with:

nginx

```nginx
server {
    listen 80;

    server_name yourdomain.com;


    location / {

        proxy_pass http://localhost:3000;

        proxy_http_version 1.1;

        proxy_set_header                Upgrade
$http_upgrade;

        proxy_set_header              Connection
'upgrade';

        proxy_set_header Host $host;

        proxy_cache_bypass $http_upgrade;

    }

}
```

3. Restart Nginx:

bash

```
sudo systemctl restart nginx
```

Your Next.js app is now live on AWS EC2.

14.4.4 Deploying to DigitalOcean

For a balance between **simplicity and flexibility**, DigitalOcean's **App Platform** is a great choice.

Step 1: Create a DigitalOcean Account

Sign up at DigitalOcean and create a new **App Platform** project.

Step 2: Deploy the Next.js App

1. Click **Create App** and choose **GitHub Repository**.

2. Select your Next.js project.

3. Configure the deployment settings:

   - **Build Command**: npm run build

   - **Start Command**: npm start

- ○ **Environment Variables**: Add `STRIPE_PUBLIC_KEY`, `DATABASE_URL`, etc.

Step 3: Enable HTTPS and Custom Domains

1. Go to **App Settings** > **Domains** and add your custom domain.

2. Enable **Automatic HTTPS** for SSL security.

Your app is now deployed on DigitalOcean.

Chapter 15: Next.js 15 Best Practices and Future Trends

As Next.js 15 continues to evolve, following best practices ensures that your applications remain **secure, efficient, and scalable**. Additionally, emerging trends such as **server components, AI integration, and edge computing** are shaping the future of web development. This chapter covers essential security measures, explores Next.js server components, examines AI-driven capabilities, and discusses upcoming trends in Next.js.

15.1 Security Best Practices for Next.js Applications

Security is a fundamental aspect of any web application, and Next.js applications are no exception. Ensuring that your application follows industry-standard security practices is crucial to protecting user data, preventing vulnerabilities, and maintaining system integrity.

This section provides a **comprehensive guide** to securing Next.js applications, covering **authentication, API security, environment management, and common attack prevention** techniques.

15.1.1 Securing API Routes

Next.js provides **API routes** that allow developers to create backend logic within the same project. However, **unprotected API routes** can be exploited if not properly secured.

Input Validation and Sanitization

SQL injection, **cross-site scripting (XSS)**, and **other injection attacks** can occur when user input is not validated or sanitized properly.

Example: Validating Input with Zod

Using zod, a TypeScript-first schema validation library, ensures that data follows the expected structure.

javascript

```javascript
import { z } from "zod";

const schema = z.object({
    username: z.string().min(3).max(20),
    email: z.string().email(),
    age: z.number().min(18)
});

export default function handler(req, res) {
    try {
        const         validatedData         =
schema.parse(req.body);
        res.status(200).json({         message:
"Valid input", data: validatedData });
    } catch (error) {
        res.status(400).json({           error:
error.errors });
    }
}
```

Key Takeaways:

- Always **validate input** before processing.

- Use **schema validation libraries** like zod, yup, or Joi.

- Reject requests with **invalid or unexpected data**.

Rate Limiting API Requests

Rate limiting protects applications from **DDoS attacks** and prevents abuse by restricting the number of requests per user.

Example: Implementing Rate Limiting in Next.js API Routes

Using express-rate-limit, you can set a maximum number of requests per time period.

javascript

```javascript
import rateLimit from "express-rate-limit";

const limiter = rateLimit({
    windowMs: 15 * 60 * 1000, // 15 minutes
    max: 100, // Limit each IP to 100 requests
    message: "Too many requests, please try
again later."
});

export default function handler(req, res) {
    limiter(req, res, () => {
        res.status(200).json({        message:
"Request allowed" });
```

```
    });
}
```

Key Takeaways:

- Prevent **brute-force attacks** and **DDoS threats** with rate limiting.

- Use `express-rate-limit` or **middleware-based solutions**.

- Implement **adaptive rate limiting** for more control.

15.1.2 Authentication and Authorization

Authentication and authorization are crucial for **restricting access** to sensitive data.

Implementing Secure Authentication

Next.js supports multiple authentication strategies, including:

- **JWT-based authentication**

- **OAuth 2.0 (Google, GitHub, Facebook)**

- **Session-based authentication with NextAuth.js**

Example: Implementing JWT Authentication

Using **jsonwebtoken (JWT)** for secure authentication:

javascript

```javascript
import jwt from "jsonwebtoken";

const secretKey = process.env.JWT_SECRET;

// Generate a token
export function generateToken(user) {
    return jwt.sign({ id: user.id, email:
user.email }, secretKey, { expiresIn: "1h" });
}

// Verify a token
export function verifyToken(token) {
    try {
        return jwt.verify(token, secretKey);
    } catch (error) {
        return null;
    }
}
```

Key Takeaways:

- **Use JWTs** to securely store authentication tokens.

- Store JWTs in **HTTP-only cookies** to prevent XSS attacks.

- Use **short-lived tokens** and refresh them periodically.

Role-Based Access Control (RBAC)

RBAC ensures that only authorized users can perform specific actions.

Example: Implementing Role-Based Access Control

javascript

```javascript
export function checkRole(user, role) {
    return user.roles.includes(role);
}

// Usage
const user = { roles: ["admin"] };
if (checkRole(user, "admin")) {
    console.log("Access granted");
} else {
    console.log("Access denied");
}
```

Key Takeaways:

- Use **RBAC to restrict access** based on user roles.

- Store **user roles in a database** and check them before processing requests.

15.1.3 Preventing Common Web Vulnerabilities

Cross-Site Scripting (XSS) Prevention

XSS occurs when **malicious scripts** are injected into a webpage.

Example: Sanitizing User Input with `sanitize-html`
javascript

```
import sanitizeHtml from "sanitize-html";

export default function handler(req, res) {
    const         sanitizedInput        =
sanitizeHtml(req.body.comment);
    res.status(200).json({ sanitizedComment:
sanitizedInput });
}
```

Key Takeaways:

- Always **sanitize user input** before displaying it on the page.

- Use `sanitize-html` **or** `DOMPurify` to prevent XSS attacks.

Cross-Site Request Forgery (CSRF) Protection

CSRF attacks exploit user authentication to perform unintended actions.

Example: Using CSRF Tokens with `csrf`
javascript

```
import csrf from "csrf";
```

496

```javascript
const tokens = new csrf();

export function generateCsrfToken() {
    return
tokens.create(process.env.CSRF_SECRET);
}

// Validate token
export function verifyCsrfToken(token) {
    return
tokens.verify(process.env.CSRF_SECRET,
token);
}
```

Key Takeaways:

- Use **CSRF tokens** to protect against forged requests.

- Store CSRF tokens in **secure cookies**.

Secure HTTP Headers

Adding **security headers** improves protection against various attacks.

Example: Configuring Headers in `next.config.js`
javascript

```javascript
module.exports = {
    async headers() {
        return [
```

```
            {
                source: "/(.*)",
                headers: [
                    { key: "X-Frame-Options",
value: "DENY" },
                    { key: "X-Content-Type-
Options", value: "nosniff" },
                    { key: "Referrer-Policy",
value: "no-referrer" },
                    { key: "Strict-Transport-
Security",     value:     "max-age=31536000;
includeSubDomains; preload" }
                ]
            }
        ];
    }
};
```

Key Takeaways:

- **Enforce HTTPS** with `Strict-Transport-Security`.

- **Prevent MIME-type sniffing** with `X-Content-Type-Options`.

- **Deny clickjacking attempts** with `X-Frame-Options`.

15.2 Exploring Next.js Server Components

Next.js 15 introduces **Server Components**, a fundamental shift in how React applications handle rendering and data fetching. Unlike traditional React components, which execute entirely on the client, **Server Components run on the server and send pre-rendered output to the client.** This architecture improves performance, reduces JavaScript bundle size, and enhances SEO.

In this section, we will explore:

- The **core differences** between Server and Client Components

- **How to create Server Components** in Next.js

- **Using Server Components for data fetching**

- **Best practices and limitations**

15.2.1 Understanding Server Components

Server Components are designed to **offload heavy computations, data fetching, and rendering tasks to the server**, ensuring that the client only receives minimal JavaScript.

Key Features of Server Components

- **No client-side JavaScript execution** – Server Components are rendered **only on the server**.

- **Smaller bundle sizes** – Since they do not include JavaScript in the client bundle, applications load faster.

- **Built-in data fetching** – Server Components can fetch data **directly from databases, APIs, or files** without exposing credentials to the client.

- **Improved SEO** – Content is pre-rendered before being sent to the client, ensuring search engines can index it efficiently.

Difference Between Server and Client Components

Feature	Server Components	Client Components
Execution	Runs on the server	Runs in the browser
JavaScript Bundling	Not included in client-side bundle	Included in the bundle
Data Fetching	Directly fetches from databases and APIs	Requires API calls from the client
Interactivity	No event listeners or hooks	Can handle user interactions, state, and events

15.2.2 Creating a Server Component

By default, **Next.js components are Server Components** unless explicitly marked as Client Components.

Example: A Simple Server Component

In `app/components/ServerComponent.js`:

javascript
```
export default async function
ServerComponent() {
```

```
    return  <h1>Welcome  to  Next.js  Server
Components</h1>;
}
```

How This Works:

- The component runs **entirely on the server**.

- The HTML output is sent to the browser **without additional JavaScript execution**.

- It **cannot use state (`useState`) or effects (`useEffect`)** because those are client-side features.

15.2.3 Fetching Data in Server Components

One of the biggest advantages of Server Components is **direct data fetching without client-side API calls**.

Example: Fetching Data from an API

javascript

```
export    default    async    function
ServerComponent() {
    const    response    =    await
fetch("https://jsonplaceholder.typicode.com/p
osts");
    const posts = await response.json();
```

```
    return (
        <div>
            <h1>Blog Posts</h1>
            <ul>
                {posts.slice(0, 5).map((post)
=> (
                    <li
key={post.id}>{post.title}</li>
                ))}
            </ul>
        </div>
    );
}
```

Key Takeaways:

- **No useEffect or state management** is needed for data fetching.

- The **data is fetched directly on the server** and sent as static HTML to the client.

- The browser **never sees the API call**—it only receives the final rendered output.

15.2.4 Mixing Server and Client Components

Not all components can be Server Components—**interactive UI elements** must still be Client Components.

Example: A Server Component Using a Client Component

Server Component (Parent):

javascript

```
import Counter from "./Counter";

export default function ServerComponent() {
    return (
        <div>
            <h1>Server Component</h1>
            <Counter />
        </div>
    );
}
```

Client Component (Child):

javascript

```
"use client";

import { useState } from "react";

export default function Counter() {
    const [count, setCount] = useState(0);

    return (
        <div>
            <p>Count: {count}</p>
            <button        onClick={()        =>
setCount(count + 1)}>Increment</button>
```

```
        </div>
    );
}
```

Key Takeaways:

- The **parent component is a Server Component** and fetches data efficiently.

- The **child component is a Client Component** and manages interactivity.

- **The `use client` directive** is required to mark a component as a Client Component.

15.2.5 Best Practices for Server Components

1. Use Server Components for Data Fetching

Fetching data in Server Components avoids unnecessary API calls in the client.

2. Minimize JavaScript in the Client

By keeping as much logic as possible in Server Components, you **reduce bundle sizes** and improve performance.

3. Avoid Using Server Components for Interactive UI Elements

Server Components **cannot handle user interactions**. Use Client Components for buttons, forms, and dynamic UI updates.

4. Leverage Server Components for SEO

Since Server Components **send fully-rendered HTML** to the browser, they **improve search engine discoverability** compared to client-side rendering.

15.3 Leveraging AI and Edge Computing in Next.js

Artificial Intelligence (AI) and Edge Computing are transforming modern web applications. Next.js 15 provides built-in support for **AI-powered applications and edge deployment**, enabling developers to build intelligent, highly scalable, and low-latency applications.

In this section, we will explore:

- **How AI and Edge Computing fit into modern Next.js applications**

- **Using AI APIs and machine learning models in Next.js**

- **Deploying AI-powered applications at the Edge**

- **Best practices for integrating AI with Edge Computing**

15.3.1 Understanding AI and Edge Computing in Next.js

What is Edge Computing?

Edge Computing **moves computation closer to the user** by running processes on distributed edge servers instead of a centralized data center. This improves **latency, speed, and scalability**.

Benefits of Edge Computing in Next.js:

- **Faster responses** – Content and computations occur closer to the user.

- **Lower bandwidth costs** – Reduces data transfers to centralized servers.

- **Better scalability** – Edge networks handle large-scale applications efficiently.

- **Enhanced security** – Reduces exposure to centralized attack points.

How Next.js Supports Edge Computing

Next.js provides **Edge Runtime support** via **Middleware and Edge API Routes**:

- **Middleware** – Processes requests at the edge before reaching the backend.

- **Edge API Routes** – Handle API requests on globally distributed edge locations.

AI in Next.js Applications

AI-powered applications can integrate **machine learning models, AI APIs, and natural language processing** to enhance user experience. Common AI use cases include:

- **Chatbots and Virtual Assistants**

- **Recommendation Engines**

- **Sentiment Analysis**

- **Automated Image and Text Processing**

Next.js can work with **serverless AI models** or **cloud AI APIs** to implement these features.

15.3.2 Integrating AI APIs in Next.js

One of the easiest ways to add AI capabilities to a Next.js application is by using AI APIs such as **OpenAI, Hugging Face, and Google Cloud AI**.

Example: Implementing an AI-powered Chatbot

This example demonstrates how to integrate **OpenAI's GPT API** to build a chatbot in Next.js.

Step 1: Install Dependencies

Run the following command to install the required package:

sh
```
npm install openai
```

Step 2: Create an API Route for AI Chat Responses

In `app/api/chat/route.js`:

javascript

```javascript
import { NextResponse } from "next/server";
import OpenAI from "openai";

const openai = new OpenAI({
    apiKey: process.env.OPENAI_API_KEY, //
Store in environment variables
});

export async function POST(req) {
    try {
        const { message } = await req.json();
        const response = await
openai.chat.completions.create({
            model: "gpt-4",
            messages: [{ role: "user",
content: message }],
        });

        return NextResponse.json({ reply:
response.choices[0].message.content });
    } catch (error) {
        return NextResponse.json({ error:
"Failed to fetch AI response" }, { status: 500
});
    }
}
```

Step 3: Create a Chat UI Component

In `app/components/Chatbot.js`:

javascript

```
"use client";
import { useState } from "react";

export default function Chatbot() {
    const [message, setMessage] =
useState("");
    const [response, setResponse] =
useState("");

    const sendMessage = async () => {
        const res = await fetch("/api/chat", {
            method: "POST",
            headers: { "Content-Type":
"application/json" },
            body: JSON.stringify({ message }),
        });

        const data = await res.json();
        setResponse(data.reply);
    };

    return (
        <div>
            <h2>AI Chatbot</h2>
            <input
                type="text"
                value={message}
```

```
                onChange={(e)                         =>
setMessage(e.target.value)}
                placeholder="Ask              me
anything..."
            />
            <button
onClick={sendMessage}>Send</button>
            <p>Response: {response}</p>
        </div>
    );
}
```

Step 4: Use the Chatbot Component

Include the chatbot in **your Next.js pages**:

javascript

```
import Chatbot from "../components/Chatbot";

export default function Home() {
    return (
        <div>
            <h1>Next.js AI Chatbot</h1>
            <Chatbot />
        </div>
    );
}
```

Key Takeaways:

- **Server-side API calls keep sensitive API keys secure.**

- **Client-side components handle user interactions**.

- **OpenAI API processes messages and returns intelligent responses**.

15.3.3 Running AI Models at the Edge

Next.js Edge Runtime enables AI inference **at globally distributed locations** using platforms like **Vercel Edge Functions** and **Cloudflare Workers**.

Deploying AI Models Using Vercel Edge Functions

Step 1: Create an Edge API Route

In `app/api/edge-ai/route.js`:

javascript

```javascript
import { NextResponse } from "next/server";
import OpenAI from "openai";

const openai = new OpenAI({
    apiKey: process.env.OPENAI_API_KEY,
});

export const config = {
    runtime: "edge", // Enable Edge Runtime
};

export async function GET(req) {
```

```
    const        response        =        await
openai.chat.completions.create({
      model: "gpt-4",
      messages: [{ role: "system", content:
"You are a helpful assistant." }],
   });

   return      NextResponse.json({      reply:
response.choices[0].message.content });
}
```

Step 2: Deploy on Vercel

- **Vercel automatically detects Edge API Routes** and deploys them to edge locations.

- The AI response **executes at the nearest edge server**, reducing latency.

Benefits of Running AI Models at the Edge

- **Faster responses** – AI inference happens close to the user.

- **Lower server costs** – Only essential logic runs on centralized servers.

- **Global scalability** – AI models serve users worldwide with minimal latency.

15.3.4 Best Practices for AI and Edge Computing in Next.js

1. Use AI for Computation-Intensive Tasks

Leverage AI for natural language processing, recommendation systems, and automation while keeping performance in mind.

2. Deploy AI Inference at the Edge When Possible

Running models at the Edge reduces **server load and response time**. Use **Vercel Edge Functions or Cloudflare Workers** when applicable.

3. Secure AI APIs and Sensitive Data

- Store API keys in **environment variables**.

- Use **server-side API routes** to call AI services instead of exposing them in client-side code.

4. Optimize AI Response Handling

AI responses should be **cached, paginated, and pre-processed** where possible to reduce redundant API calls.

15.4 What's Next for Next.js?

Next.js 15 represents a major step forward in **modern web development**, but the framework is constantly evolving to meet the demands of developers and businesses. In this section, we will explore:

- Upcoming features and innovations in Next.js

- The role of AI and automation in future Next.js development

- How Next.js is shaping the future of full-stack applications

- What developers should focus on to stay ahead

15.4.1 The Future of Next.js Development

Next.js has continuously evolved from a **React-based static site generator** to a **full-stack web development framework** with support for **server-side rendering (SSR), React Server Components (RSC), and edge computing**. The next phase of its evolution will focus on:

- **Enhanced performance optimizations** with better caching and streaming.

- **AI-powered development workflows** to automate repetitive tasks.

- **More seamless integration with cloud services** for serverless applications.

- **Continued improvements in developer experience** through simplified APIs and tools.

15.4.2 Expected Features and Improvements

While specific upcoming changes depend on the roadmap set by the **Vercel team and Next.js contributors**, trends in the framework's development suggest the following advancements:

1. Deeper AI Integration

AI is playing a bigger role in **developer productivity and application functionality**. Next.js is expected to introduce:

- **AI-assisted code generation** for components, pages, and API routes.

- **Intelligent caching and performance suggestions** based on application behavior.

- **Prebuilt AI-powered components** for common use cases like chatbots, recommendations, and automation.

2. More Granular Server-Side Rendering (SSR) Control

Current SSR strategies are **optimized but still require careful tuning**. Future versions of Next.js will likely introduce:

- **Dynamic SSR optimizations** to determine when pages should be rendered on the server or cached at the edge.

- **Hybrid rendering approaches** that intelligently mix static generation, incremental static regeneration (ISR), and server rendering based on traffic patterns.

3. Next-Generation API Handling

API development in Next.js continues to improve, with potential future enhancements including:

- **Edge-first API routes** that automatically determine whether a function should run at the edge or a traditional server.

- **Improved middleware for handling authentication, security, and request validation**.

- **Enhanced GraphQL support** with built-in optimizations for real-time data fetching.

4. Streamlined Deployment and CI/CD Integration

Deploying and maintaining Next.js applications is becoming more **automated and efficient**. Future improvements may include:

- **One-click deployment and rollback mechanisms** with better version control.

- **Optimized CI/CD workflows** that detect changes and apply only necessary updates.

- **Advanced monitoring and debugging tools** for performance insights at a deeper level.

15.4.3 Next.js and the Future of Full-Stack Development

Next.js is driving the **future of full-stack JavaScript applications** by making it easier to build, scale, and deploy high-performance applications. Key trends include:

1. The Rise of Full-Stack React Development

- With Next.js leading the **React ecosystem**, developers no longer need separate front-end and back-end frameworks.

- Features like **React Server Components and API Routes** enable **seamless integration** of UI and business logic.

2. Serverless and Edge Computing as the Default

- Next.js is shifting towards **serverless-first architectures**, allowing developers to focus on **writing code instead of managing infrastructure**.

- **Edge functions and middleware** make applications more responsive and scalable without additional configuration.

3. Component-Based Development for Everything

- The future of Next.js is **deeply tied to reusable, optimized components**.

- **Design systems and component libraries** will be critical for building scalable applications efficiently.

15.4.4 How to Stay Ahead as a Next.js Developer

To remain at the **forefront of Next.js development**, developers should:

1. Follow the Next.js Roadmap

- Stay updated with **Vercel's official announcements and Next.js releases**.

- Participate in **community discussions and open-source contributions**.

2. Learn and Experiment with AI-Powered Features

- Explore how AI can **automate workflows, optimize rendering, and enhance user experiences**.

- Experiment with **AI-driven code generation and predictive caching**.

3. Master Edge Computing and Serverless Architectures

- Learn **how to deploy APIs and applications at the edge** for improved performance.

- Optimize applications for **cost efficiency and scalability** using **serverless functions and dynamic rendering**.

4. Understand New Patterns in API Development

- Stay up to date with **GraphQL, WebSockets, and streaming APIs** for real-time applications.

- Master **Next.js middleware and API routes** to build **secure and scalable full-stack applications**.

5. Improve Performance Optimization Skills

- Master techniques like **lazy loading, code splitting, and caching strategies**.

- Optimize **database queries and API responses** for better performance.

www.ingramcontent.com/pod-product-compliance
Lightning Source LLC
LaVergne TN
LVHW081508050326
832903LV00025B/1417